Honorée Corder
Author, *Vision to Reality & Business Dating*

The Divorced Phoenix
Rising from the Ashes of a Broken Marriage

The end of your marriage can be the beginning of a whole new you. This is a book about how to start your amazing transformation, right now.

Published by Honorée Enterprises Publishing, LLC.

Copyright 2016 ©Honorée Enterprises Publishing, LLC & Honorée Corder

ISBN: 978-0-9961861-5-5

Discover other titles by Honorée Corder at
http://www.honoreecorder.com.

Additional titles by Honorée Corder

Tall Order! Organize Your Life and Double Your Success in Half the Time (10th Anniversary Edition)

Prosperity for Writers: A Writer's Guide to Creating Abundance

Prosperity for Writers Productivity Journal: A Writer's Workbook to Creating Abundance

Business Dating: Applying Relationship Rules in Business for Ultimate Success

Vision to Reality: How Short Term Massive Action Equals Long Term Maximum Results

If Divorce is a Game, These are the Rules: 8 Rules for Thriving Before, During and After Divorce

The Successful Single Mom

The Successful Single Mom Cooks! Cookbook

The Successful Single Mom Gets Rich!

The Successful Single Mom Finds Love

The Successful Single Mom Gets Fit!

The Successful Single Mom Gets an Education

Madre Soltera y Exitosa

Play to Pay: How to Market Your College-Bound Student-Athlete for Scholarship Money

Paying for College: How to Save 25-50% on Your Child's College Education

The Successful Single Dad

Table of Contents

A Note from the Author

I had no idea when my ex-husband returned home after a nine-month military deployment and asked for a divorce what my future would hold. If you had asked me in that moment to predict if it was the end or the beginning, I would surely have said, THE END. And, I might have thrown in "*game over*" for good measure.

In *If Divorce is a Game*, I shared my strategies and ideas for navigating the divorce process with as much ease and grace as possible. This book is about the next phase of life.

If you are entering Year Three, which means your divorce was final two or more years ago, you have officially entered the next phase of your life, a time when you have most likely healed the majority of your wounds and begun to feel more like yourself again. But you might be wondering, who the heck am I? What do I want to do with the rest of my life? You might have a handle on your professional path, but a personal path might be a mystery. And you might be wondering if, just maybe, you'll find someone new. Is love a possibility?

My friend, I am here to tell you that the answers to the above questions are full of hope, possibility, opportunity, and a maximum amount of positivity!

This period of your life is a clean slate. You can paint upon this canvas an assortment of goodies that exist on an endless list of potentiality.

While you may still harbor some hurt and have some healing to do, the future is yours.

Even if you're still not quite divorced, this book holds inspiration, wisdom and tools you can use to design your future.

If you're ready, let's do this!

Honorée Corder
Divorcée, Wife, Writer, Coach, Mom

Introduction

Anyone who has gone through a divorce knows there's a period of time when survival is pretty much the only goal. The numbness has worn off, and the pain from a nonphysical event feels all too real. But it raises the question: Is it possible to thrive after divorce instead of merely surviving?

That was the question I asked myself as I navigated through the stages of grief after my divorce. Never one to settle, I wanted to stop feeling okay and start feeling great. I wanted to learn the lessons I was supposed to learn, lest I become destined to repeat them, and expand into a bigger and better life for my daughter and myself.

I realized that in order to thrive, I needed to embrace my new life rather than resist it. My divorce became an opportunity for growth instead of a pronounced failure or worse, a death sentence. So I embarked on a transformation that was equally exciting and painful at times, but completely worth it! The period of time during and after my divorce led me to what is now a large portion of my life's work: helping people transform after divorce. The *Single Mom*

Transformation Program was created from my work as an executive coach, and *The Successful Single Mom* book series (as well as *The Successful Single Dad*) was born so that others could create their own powerful, positive transformation. Eventually, I wrote *If Divorce is a Game, These Are the Rules* as a guidebook to help people learn the secrets to navigating the process of divorce so that everyone wins.

If you are ready to embark on your post-divorce transformation, you're in for some hard work, but the reward is a major treat called *your new life*. This can be the beginning of some of the very best years of your life, if you will allow them to be!

Thriving after divorce isn't impossible, au contraire, it's actually very possible. You can do it by starting today and recommitting to the new life you're creating every day.

The Divorced Phoenix is the book to get your transformation well under way. Are you ready? Let's go!

Your future is yours. If you're ready to create it, take the first step. You've got this!

Chapter One:
The Rise of the Phoenix: YOU

If you jump into the fire, you will come out in the water. If you jump into the water, you will come out in the fire.
—Rumi

In a perfect world, you would have stayed married to the love of your life. But for any number of reasons, that marriage has ended. We don't live in a perfect world, but in case you haven't been told or given a peek behind the curtain, there are happily divorced people. The majority of divorced people I've spoken to over the years agree that their divorces were painful in varying degrees, and they also wouldn't change the outcome for the world. Their divorces allowed them to discover a happy life and sides of themselves they might otherwise have missed.

I call theses happy divorcées *Divorced Phoenixes.*

Let's take a moment and start with, *What is a phoenix?* In ancient stories, a phoenix is a magical bird that lives for 500 years before it dies in a show of flames, only to be born again from its ashes.

A Divorced Phoenix, then, is a person who has risen from the ashes of their previous marriage. They have turned a painful situation into a brand new life.

You may feel as though you have definitely gone through the dying and flames part and have not yet risen from the ashes. I promise you the best is yet to come, if you let it. You will need to facilitate your transition with intention and purpose. My aim is to walk with you into the beginning of your prodigious future, encouraging you to keep going, to not only design it, but also to let it come about sooner.

In *If Divorce is a Game*, I focused on the *how to* of divorcing in a way that everyone can come through with their self-esteem and sanity intact. I didn't do more than forecast a fantastic future for you. *The Divorced Phoenix* is here to make sure you know that an incredible life is just around the corner and that you can put the full force of your intention behind creating it.

Because I don't want any residual emotions or feelings sneaking up on you when you least expect it, there is one more stop on your past history train. I would be remiss if I didn't encourage you to dot your i's and cross your t's before revealing how to lean into all of the goodies and goodness on your horizon. Come with me for a short time to a place you'll have to visit sooner or later. Let's make sure our bags are appropriately packed for the journey ahead, shall we?

The Power of Forgiveness

You're like me, I can feel it, and neither of us wants to spend one minute more than is absolutely necessary in the past. Holding on to what might have been, or even the tiniest of grudges, could impede something amazing. But if you don't stop long enough to take care of necessary business, you might find yourself overcome with emotions you won't enjoy.

If you haven't yet forgiven all involved parties (yes, *forgiven* your ex, any other people who may or may not have been involved in the demise of your former matrimony ... and yourself), please forgive them with your whole heart and soul as soon as possible. Don't wait another minute to do it.

You might be thinking, *How the #@$! am I supposed to do that, Honorée? You don't know my situation, and frankly, the entire thing, what happened to me, is completely unforgiveable.*

I understand better than you might think how hard it is to forgive, forget, and start moving on. It can be incredibly hard to let go, especially because a marriage comes with the expectation that it will last forever. You may think it's easier to stay mad, try to get revenge, lick your wounds, and feel sorry for yourself.

Listen to me now: you deserve better than to wear your divorce on your sleeve and your face. You deserve better than to let residual negative emotions eat you alive, stealing away your happiness and joy. Don't let what happened yesterday ruin the incredible future in store for you.

If you think people can't see and feel your divorce on you, you're wrong. They can, until you make a decision to forgive and move forward.

For reasons I think everyone would understand, I'm not going to talk too much about the catalysts for my own divorce (not the least of which is because my amazing daughter may someday read this). You can rest assured I have several reasons to continue harboring homicidal tendencies. But that wouldn't do anyone any good at all, most of all myself and my daughter. So here I sit, fourteen years later, with only a healthy respect for my previous marriage and all parties involved. I also have a deep appreciation for all that has come to me because I not only survived it, but have thrived in many ways because of it.

I may not be the original Divorced Phoenix, but I definitely am one. And I want you to be one, too.

Think of holding a grudge this way: You drink the poison and expect your ex (and possibly others) to die. Seems silly when I put it that way, right? Holding a grudge is like playing hot potato, but instead of passing it on, you're clinging on to it to the point where it inflicts a third-degree burn. Your ex is out there living their life, and you sit in suffering. How can that even be a real thing? I believe any further suffering is optional. The question is, do you?

If you're ready to forgive and move on, to do what needs to be done and go forward, there's no better time than the present, right?

Let's rock this forgiveness thing. I've got the six steps you need to do it:

1. **Write down the name of the person you need to forgive and the gist of their transgression.** No need to go into great detail. That will only serve to upset you and perhaps prevent you from taking the next steps.

2. **Ask for help.** Call on a power bigger than yourself. *Lord, I can't forgive* ___ *without your help. Please help me to forgive.* No religion involved here if that's not your thing. Ask the universe or some higher or larger power you believe in to assist.

3. **Have a realization.** Realize this: If you can be forgiven for everything you've ever done (with or to this person or to someone else), forgiveness in this situation is also possible. No one is fault-free in any situation, least of all a divorce ... this includes you. As you forgive, so shall you be forgiven.

4. **Surrender.** There's nothing that can be done about the past, and that makes now the time to give up any desire to get revenge. You will feel good when you just let it all go. I suggest writing down your hurts, or your hatred, frustration, and/or sadness, and any desire you have

for revenge. Put all of the ugliness on paper, and then set it on fire. Watch them burn, and let the feelings that accompany those thoughts leave you just as the smoke rises up from the fire.

5. **Bless the forgiven.** The act of giving a blessing is incredibly powerful, and can mean giving approval or asking for protection. In your situation, both may be needed. Mentally bless the person who has hurt you. This is the act of not only wishing them well, but also giving your approval for them and for yourself.

6. **Release them to their highest good.** What we wish for others actually comes back to us, multiplied. Let your former spouse go into their future with your best wishes, and what will come to you will only be good things.

Feel better yet? I hope so! The above process of forgiveness and letting go with a positive intention will be good for you and bring good things to you. If you're not feeling better quite yet, stick with it. In time, you can forgive and release the past to move toward your exciting, new future. I know when someone is willing to do the work of forgiveness, they are also ready to move forward with their transformation. That's what this book is all about: the incredible life that follows a truly possible, yet currently inconceivable, transformation.

The 5 Stages of Grief and Loss

Depending on how long you have been officially divorced, you may or may not have traversed all of the stages of grief and loss. It is my understanding that they were never meant to bundle all the messy emotions of divorce into neat little packages. Each stage is an emotional response that most people have when they encounter a traumatic event, such as divorce. But make no mistake, there is no typical response to the loss of a marriage. Indeed, our grief and our feelings of loss are as individual as we are.

The five stages, denial, anger, bargaining, depression, and (finally) acceptance, are part of the framework that helps us to make sense of our life and our feelings after divorce. In essence, these stages help us identify where we are in the grieving process, and contain within them the tools to help us move through our feelings and into the next stage. Unfortunately, going through the stages of grief is not like taking the subway from 42nd St. to Madison Square Garden. The stages are neither linear nor do they come in any particular order. My hope is that you find yourself firmly planted in the acceptance stage with this book in your hands. However, if by chance you're not sure, here is a brief overview of each of the stages and a description or two that will help you recognize that stage in yourself, in case it's helpful.

Denial. Denial, otherwise known as shock, is an automatic response we have when a situation is beyond our comprehension. When thrust into denial, we wonder, in layman's terms, "what the hell?" But denial is nature's way of gracefully giving us the time we need to adjust to the fact that a senseless, overwhelming, or severely painful change has occurred in our life.

Anger. Without question, you may sail through denial only to find yourself smack dab in the midst of a righteous anger. And make no mistake; this is not the time to pretend you're not livid. If you deny your anger, it only grows. When you're mad, really embrace the fact that you have your mad on. Soon you will have passed through it.

Underneath the anger is great pain. Anger is the structure you use to deal with the pain. Connecting with your anger most likely feels better than succumbing to overwhelming sadness. The angrier you are, the deeper your feelings of love and, simultaneously, hurt. With time, these intense feelings will lessen, and then you'll move on to ...

Bargaining. During the bargaining phase, you may find, or have found, that you have an almost irrational desire to forgive and forget. It doesn't matter that your spouse has another wife and children or that your bride has taken up with your brother. In this stage, you will do almost anything to retreat into your previous life of blissful unawareness. In this stage, we tend to blame ourselves for the entire situation, even if our complete and total responsibility is minimal.

Depression. After we realize we cannot negotiate our way back into bliss, our attention focuses solely on today, the present. It is not uncommon for the depression stage to manifest as intense sadness and a complete retreat from the outside world. This phase will not last forever: the fog will eventually lift, and you will move on to the next stage, which is (finally) ...

Acceptance. While you may not ever be okay with how your marriage ended, what was said, or what went on, at some point you will accept that it is what it is. You will learn to live with it, and you will accept your new normal. Once you are officially, and finally, in this stage you are poised for what is about to happen next!

And, ladies and gentlemen, it is soooooo good! I promise you!

Let the Transformation Begin!

The rise of the phoenix starts with a decision. In this case, the decision you make changes the course of your life: *I'm deciding to make the best of my divorce instead of letting my divorce get the better of me.*

This decision to move forward into the unknown with only a sliver of hope and some positive expectation begins the path to resurrection, the realization you have an indestructible spirit, and your transformation.

The decision is simple—all you have to do is make it. What to decide is first and foremost. I suggest deciding to allow all of the magical and miraculous happenings, people, and adventures into your life ... as soon as possible!

In my pursuit of personal growth and professional expansion, I've read hundreds, if not thousands, of personal growth books. They all seem to suggest that once you decide to erase your perceived limits on happiness, success, and abundance, those very things will rush into your life so quickly you'll hardly believe it. The flood of fabulosity is so great it stands to reason the good-in-waiting was right there all along, just waiting for the "Go!"

Your Steps into Greatness

It is entirely possible your goodies might take a few minutes (weeks or months) to show up in their entirety. While you're waiting, take these steps into greatness. They might help you get to your new, amazing life faster, and will definitely help you enjoy the journey.

Appreciate. I'm always looking for the shortest, fastest, most effective and efficient way to get something done. Is it because I'm prone to laziness? I'll never tell. But during my journey from post-divorce pity party into my transformation, I happened upon an exercise I know you will enjoy: *Write down everything you're grateful for whether it relates to your divorce or not.*

I'll get you started: I'm grateful to be alive. I'm grateful to be able to write and read these words (my eyes work, thank goodness!). I'm grateful for my spirit that never quits. I'm grateful for my daughter, current husband, health, businesses, clients, home, car ... The list is almost endless. I'm grateful for the gifts my divorce gave me, which are too many to mention, but here's a biggie: the ability to help you after your divorce.

Before you continue, make your list.

Recommit. Your new life post-divorce is not "one day life sucks and the next day life suddenly rocks." Nope. In fact, each day you must be prepared to recommit to your happiness and success. Until you are fully living your new life—complete with any or all of the following: new love, new work, new friends, and a new place to live (for starters)— there are gonna be good days and not so good days. On the good days, it is easy to see that your divorce was a full-on blessing and you can't imagine life any other way. Some days you're going to think to yourself, "How the heck did I end up here? And why?!" It is entirely up to you to see the blessings even when they are in disguise, and continue to be on the lookout (BOLO) for the wonderful things coming down the pike. The list of things you appreciate will definitely help you to recommit to creating your new life.

Respond. You are not a victim, and being in the midst of a transformation you never asked for does not make you one. Today, and each day that follows, provides an opportunity to respond instead of react to what is happening to you and around you. Each event is either great or is clearing the way for something great. Take a step back whenever life is most definitely not to your liking and decide what you will allow it to mean to you. No event or thing has a meaning other than the one you give to it.

Envision. The old vision you had of your life is something you've had to let go of, and that was no easy task, I'm sure (it wasn't for me). We're going to talk about this in more detail, but I want you to start to imagine a vibrant, healthy, delightful, and joy-filled vision that gets you excited just thinking about it. Excited people thrive, it's a fact, and it's time for you to be one of them.

Let's get this party—your new party—started!

Moving On:
Your Action Steps for Moving Forward

✓ Do your forgiveness work. You'll be so glad you did!

✓ Identify the stage you're in right now. Write it down, and prepare yourself for what's next.

✓ Make your decision! Something like, *My transformation starts now!*

✓ Take your steps into greatness. It's time!

The Divorced Phoenix

Chapter Two:
Your New Beginning

*New beginnings are often disguised as
painful endings.* —Lao Tzu

There is no future in holding on to the past. Once you've come to terms with the lessons and the blessings of your marriage, it is time to step fully into the process of defining an amazing future for yourself.

Just because your marriage ended in divorce doesn't mean there weren't some amazing times and also some incredible lessons and insights you can use to your advantage as you move into the future.

I hate having to learn a lesson more than once. But if you're a slow learner like I am sometimes, it helps to put down what I'm supposed to be learning (or have learned) in black and white. Mostly so I can stare at it until I really get it.

Because your marriage and the particulars of it are probably still fresh in your mind, let's do a quick exercise you may find beneficial for a long time to come.

Lessons Learned List

Because you most likely do not want to repeat any painful situations that occurred during your marriage, it is helpful to do some reflection. I tend to reflect best when I have specific questions to answer, and you might as well. In your journal, do your best to answer these questions:

1. What were your biggest positive takeaways from your marriage?

2. What were you great at in your marriage?

3. What could you have done better?

4. If you had it to do all over again, what would you do differently?

5. If time, space, money, and even age were no object, describe how would you describe your ideal future life, career, and relationships?

I didn't want to say this beforehand, but answering those questions takes a tremendous amount of courage. And if you're still reading and haven't answered those questions yet, I understand why. I encourage you to answer them and to be gentle with yourself if the answers don't come easily or come too easily and you don't like them very much. The transformative process you are embarking upon is not for sissies. To truly transform takes guts, heart, and some grit. Not everyone is up to the task, but everyone who takes it is damn glad they did. So if you are wavering, wondering if you should push forward when it's tough to do so, or if you should retreat to the safety of your cocoon, picture me sitting with you in a quaint café somewhere lovely (Paris, perhaps?) saying just the right things to keep you going.

Once you have answered the questions, and learned what you can from your experience, I have great news I have to share with you. It is time to define a new and exciting vision for yourself.

Defining a New Vision

Having done the work of forgiveness and identified your lessons learned, you are now perfectly poised to craft the vision of your life. When you're in a marriage, happy or not, the vision you are likely to have and to hold is an *us* vision, not a *me* vision. Today, my friend, the vision you are crafting of your future belongs to you and you alone. I have been very happily remarried for seven years, and my husband and I most definitely have a *we* vision. But even as I am writing this, I'm getting very excited for you! Mostly because there was a time when I got to do this very exercise for myself, and now, not only am I living the very best vision I could have conceived for myself at the time, the life I currently live is so much better. Now I don't say that to try to impress you. The reason my happy life is important to you is because I found its beginnings first in the visioning process I'm about to share with you.

To borrow a bit from my book *Tall Order!*, a vision is what you see in your mind's eye today, but it's not necessarily something you're able to see in reality quite yet. Your vision is the picture you have in your mind when you think of a desired outcome. Think for just a moment what your future could be like if it were truly amazing, a life in which you woke up every day and had to pinch yourself because everything was just so good.

To create your vision, I want you to start with daydreaming. Imagine what your life would look like with no boundaries. If you have a moment of pause that includes the thought, *that is impossible for me*, do me a favor—no, do yourself a favor—and suspend disbelief entirely. Put a lid on your perceived limitations and allow yourself to think as big as you possibly can. Shall we continue?

What are the areas of your life where, up to this point, you've been playing either too small, or not big enough? Have you put mental limitations on how healthy or fit you can be, how much money you can make, how much you can achieve, or how far you can travel by yourself? What areas of your life aren't working as well as you would like them to? As you identify each area, write a few sentences (or even a few paragraphs) about how you would like to see them. But here's the trick: write them in the positive and in the present tense as though right now you were living as you would like to be living in the future.

Instead of writing, "I see myself losing 25 pounds," you might want to write, "I am so happy and grateful to be vibrantly healthy at 135 (or 180) pounds."

If you are looking at the future with a wary eye, I get it. I do understand how hard it is to look at the future with exuberance and enthusiasm if you are still doing a bit of healing. But let me be the first to give you little tough love (okay, maybe not the first) and remind you that your attitude determines your altitude. In other words, people tend to get what they expect, and if you're expecting more [insert negative emotion here], you will get more of that. Remember I've asked you to completely suspend disbelief. If you're thinking that your past experiences are an accurate predictor of your future experiences, then you might be a tad skeptical or cynical about just how happy you can possibly be. And because I know the example of just one person, me, wouldn't be enough to convince you that a happy life after divorce is not only possible, but probable, I've included many stories in the last chapter of this book from people just like you (and me) who are thriving after divorce. (It's okay to skip to the end for some encouragement, but then come on back and pick up where you left off.)

I hope by now you've begun to pencil in even the slightest sketch of the life you'd like to live. I'd like to add one more element to the phrase "your attitude determines your altitude." There is a big difference between hoping something is going to happen and being absolutely certain it's going to happen. A person who is certain something is going to happen carries themselves with the positive energy that everyone around them can feel. When you're only able to hope something is going to happen, you also hold the option in your mind that it might not happen. Hope provides for two distinctly different outcomes. Certainty allows for only one, and I submit to you that if you're going to be certain about anything, you should become certain that the vision you're creating is what you'll actually be living in fairly short order. I'm gonna talk more about how to do that in the next chapter, so for right now, let me say this: You are in the driver's seat from this day forward. You get to make 100 percent of the decisions affecting your happiness and your future.

I've got a whole chapter for you on creating your vision. So if you don't have one right now, it's all good. We'll get there. But first it's time for a change in who tops your priority list.

Moving On:
Your Action Steps for Moving Forward

✓ Make a Lessons Learned List.

✓ Define, or begin to define, your new vision for your life.

The Divorced Phoenix

Chapter Three:
A New Number One: YOU

It's time to be selfish. Put yourself first,
and you become an example to others
for how to treat you.

You might be wondering if I'm going to tell you the quickest, easiest, and best way to go from where you are now straight into a new, fantastic life. Why yes, yes I am!

The next step in the *I want a great new life* process is both the simplest, and perhaps the hardest piece of the puzzle, and it is this: You have to take 100% ownership and stewardship over your future happiness and develop the attitude it takes to get there. The new number one in your life is ... (drum roll please) ... YOU!

From now on you can't, not even once, allow any other person to influence your attitude in a negative way or steal your joy. Not even for a second. Your unshakable positive attitude will be tested from all angles, and you may find it hard, from time to time, to stay the course.

Putting yourself first, becoming your new number one, is going to require some circumstantial navigation, a bucketful of chutzpah, and a whole lot of selective hearing. And, because you never know when one of these challenging situations is going to arise, the best defense is a good offense.

What follows is a complete list of action steps you can take to fortify your spirit, step up your resolve, head off trials and tribulations at the pass, and help you turn that carefully crafted vision into your present-day, real-life reality.

Mental Malpractice

You might be guilty of performing something I have termed "mental malpractice." I define this term as the deliberate misuse of our mental faculties and capabilities. Don't worry, we're all guilty of mental malpractice from time to time. Most likely every person who has just finalized their divorce has found themselves more susceptible to negative thoughts, snide comments and sarcasm. Or was that just me? (I didn't think so.)

If you have ever caught yourself saying or thinking something negative (ahem), these four steps will help you to master your mindset, turn the beat around, and stop committing mental malpractice for good.

1. Develop a no whining policy. When my daughter was three, we lived in an apartment. She attended a pre-school, where I'm assuming she picked up the fine art of whining. So, one morning I took her outside and showed her our apartment number and told her that it said, "No whining inside." She was free to sit outside on the steps if she wanted to whine, but inside she needed to use her big girl voice and ask for what she wanted (and be sure to say "please" along with it). Long ago, I developed a no whining policy. Why? Because that shiznit just doesn't work. Whining is annoying, unproductive, and frankly, might even instigate a bitch slap. Perhaps I might change this to a "no tolerance for whining" policy. Some days I might feel like whining, but I know it won't help. Instead, I decide what I want and state that, sometimes to myself, sometimes to someone else. And I always include a "please," because manners help. If you've been prone to whining in the past, I highly encourage you to stop, and instead, decide what you want and ask nicely for it.

2. Focus solely on what you want and nothing else. If you're focusing on what's going wrong, know this: what you're focusing on gets bigger. Once you've defined a new vision, you can also create a mini-movie in your mind, a "moving visualization" of what you want to create, to go along with it. By all means, turn off the news. You don't need to see all that negativity, do you? Instead, use the power of your subconscious mind to effortlessly draw your desired vision to you. Close your eyes and visualize your goals and vision as if you've already achieved them. Get acquainted with how you will feel once you start living the new life you have mentally crafted for yourself. (Hint: it feels amazing!) Once you've determined where you are (your "point A"), your best approach to find success is to focus on the strategies and solutions for making your vision a reality. Stay in solution mode by focusing on how you can make it happen and what options you have. What does that mean? It means to look solely for the solution to a problem or situation. Whether you are looking for a problem or solution, you will surely find it, so turn up the volume on your can-do voice, and seek out the ways to get 'er done.

3. Be grateful. Make time for gratitude each day. Even just a few moments spent contemplating all the good things in your life will bring a positive shift to your entire day. Give thanks for everyone and everything in your life that you are thankful for. Obtain a journal if you don't have one already and create a running list of everything you're grateful for and about. When you connect with gratitude, your fear will simply fade away. Adopt the belief that "every day above ground is a great day." It's true, using gratitude to eliminate fear is a real thing. If you're reading this, then you're still here, and that's a good thing! There's still the possibility for you to have, do, be, and create anything and everything you truly want. Your fastest path from here to there begins with an extra-large scoop of gratitude.

4. Set a time limit for complaining, and adopt "Can't change it!" as your mantra. Hal Elrod, a mindset master, author of *The Miracle Morning*, and one of my favorite people, has a cool and effective mindset strategy that really works. Give yourself five minutes or less to "vent, moan, or complain" about a situation that's got your goat. Get it all out and say everything you need to say. Then say, out loud, "Can't change it!" and move on.

In the movie, *Bridge of Spies* (with the amazing Tom Hanks), an old man is on trial for being a Russian spy. After Tom Hanks paints a bleak and horrid picture for the old man, he comments, "You don't seem worried about this situation you find yourself in." The old man wisely replies, "Would it help?" In other words, getting all spun up, bent out of shape, and *staying that way* won't in any way change your situation. In fact, those negative emotions can actually damage you. So pretend they are a hot lava rock and let 'em go.

With the four strategies I've shared above (and I highly suggest you dog-ear or bookmark these pages for easy reference), you can master your mindset starting today and keep ahold of it during all of your tomorrows. It starts with a decision, your decision to go for it. I think you're gonna love your new Zen attitude...

Mental Ninja Tricks

I've just finished telling you that you're practically bulletproof, and now I'm going to offer you some more tricks. What gives? Well, the last I checked you're human, and we humans can use all the help we can get.

When all else fails, here are some extra-fabulous mental ninja tricks to keep you going in the right direction.

- **Ask yourself some better questions.** Try these: "What's great about this?" or "What has to happen to make this situation the way that I want it?" For goodness sake, people, do not ask, "What else can go wrong?" Instead, ask yourself, "How can this day get better?"

- **Get moving!** Emotion is created from motion, so get moving. Sitting on the couch chowing down on a box of Oreos isn't productive (so I've heard) and will not help you one single bit. After you realize you "can't change it," you'll notice that there is something you can change: what you are physically doing. When you need to change your energy or focus or shake off a bad mood, do what I do: go for a walk. Bonus: listen to something positive like an inspiring podcast, an audiobook, or your workout playlist (at all costs, avoid Adele, as much as I love her). You probably won't need more than about ten minutes to shift yourself back into a positive mental state.

- **Have faith.** Sometimes the only thing you can do is know that you've survived all the challenging times you've faced so far, and that fact will help you realize that you'll survive what is happening right now, too. The sun will come out tomorrow, and at any moment, you can have the breakthrough you're looking for.

• **Remember, "be, do, and then have."** You must be positive, and then do the right things to have (get) what you want. To be enthusiastic, you must decide to be enthusiastic and fake it until you make it.

• **Shift and the world shifts with you.** Decide that today is going to be an awesome day, expect it to be awesome, and plant yourself firmly in a field of positive expectation. Ask yourself: What great thing is going to happen next?

• **When something less-than-fantastic happens, you have a choice to respond or react.** Reacting very often involves an adrenaline rush along with anger or frustration rearing their ugly heads. Choose instead to respond in whatever way is appropriate, reference the other tools I've shared, and then press the reset button on your attitude.

• **Dedicate yourself daily (hourly, if necessary) to expanding the scope of your positive attitude.** A positive mental attitude is a choice, a daily choice, and one you are entirely capable of making. Sometimes you just have to decide you're going to be the most positive person you encounter all day.

- **Think positive. Read positive. Listen positive. Talk positive. Affirm positive. Watch positive. Practice positive. Make yourself positive. Every single day.**

BOLO!

I believe some people have a *now* setting or a *later* setting. I definitely have the now setting, which means when it's time to start doing something, the time is usually right now. Chances are, you'll want to start your transformation right now, so I'm going to give you a tool you can start using this moment. You can use this tool in conjunction with your new mental mindset tools, and you will be a force of unstoppable awesomesauce.

I'm sure you have watched one of the thousands of police dramas on television. After a crime, a witness describes the fleeing suspect. (He was about 5'11"! Brown hair! Red Baseball cap!) The detective will then say, *"Let's put out a BOLO on the suspect."* "BOLO" is an acronym for be on the lookout.

I don't use BOLO in the traditional pursuit-of-criminal sense. I've adopted the term BOLO for use on my own transformational journey. If you want to turn your vision into reality, the first step is to notice all of the other people who are doing the same thing you want to do. Guess what? Divorced folks who have transformed their lives surround you, but you might not have noticed them quite yet. While you were navigating your divorce, you might have noticed others who were going through the same thing, were smack-dab in the middle of an unhappy marriage, or even at the beginning of their breakup. But now that you're on the edge of your transformation, you are going to intentionally BOLO and notice who around you is doing what they love, earning money from their passion, in a relationship with someone wonderful, or living in the home of their dreams, in spite of having gone through a divorce. You get my point here, right?

An abundance of what we want to bring into our lives surrounds us every day. But, if you haven't been looking for it, you probably haven't noticed it. Makes sense, right?

Pull out your journal and write down every instance you can think of where you know of someone doing what they want to be doing (Taking trips, starting a new business, going on fun dates, redecorating their home). Right now I'm obsessed with London. I can't wait to go, and I even have a trip planned in a few months! I'm constantly seeing London on the news, and talking to people who live in London, have visited

London, or are from London. I even got an issue of a travel magazine, the London Issue, as a gift from client. I have a friend from London, and of course, I see her posts in my Facebook feed every morning.

Because I'm on the lookout for what I want, I see reminders of it everywhere. You will, too!

What you want is an abundance of post-divorce happiness, correct? Okay then, here's what I want you to look for and make note of: All of the people you see (those you know and those you don't) who are thriving and having a great time after divorce. On Facebook alone, I have two recently divorced friends who have their arms wrapped around their own transformations. I promise, once you start looking, you'll notice them everywhere!

My friend Kathleen went through a divorce last year, and this year she's starting to feel like herself again. She's getting in shape and posting pictures of her sweaty after-workout pictures. She's hired a trainer and is becoming more fit and strong every day. She looks amazing, and she's glowing. She's fully embraced her post-divorce transformation, and it shows!

Another friend, Rob, is a professional narrator. Even though he experienced a life-threatening health challenge recently, the year since his divorce has been pretty great. In the last few months alone, he's gotten more jobs than in the previous three years and has signed with a top-level agent. His career trajectory has skyrocketed, and he's more positive and hopeful than ever.

Those are just the people I know, and I'm not even going through a divorce! Maybe I'm on high alert because I already have a book on divorce and I'm writing this one. My point is, you can turn on your *reticular activator*, the part of your brain that notices what you tell it to notice, and see things you might otherwise have missed.

Take a few minutes to appreciate the similarities between you and the people you've noticed that are living it up after divorce. Let me remind you that these folks are just a bit further along the path than you are. You might not feel like going to the gym on a regular basis quite yet, but you can probably imagine how great Katherine feels, and how great you'd feel if you did the same. Let the people like Katherine that you see in your own life provide inspiration for your own transformation.

You might not have found your professional passion yet, so finding yours and making it a reality like Rob has done may seem out of reach. I promise you it isn't! Your only job right now is to BOLO for those that are having, doing, and being what you want. The rest will come, I assure you.

Throughout this book, I'm going to give you more tools, action steps, and yes, more homework. I know you will feel better as I share (and you implement) these tangible steps, so they are headed your way. Sound good?

As a coach, I always assign tasks to my clients. Each one means something and has a specific purpose—though they may sometimes feel more like "wax on, wax off" from *The Karate Kid* than something that makes immediate sense. It might not seem like there's a method to my madness, but I assure you there is. Set aside any hesitations or resistance you might have and at least give 'em a try. You truly don't have anything to lose and everything to gain.

As a side note, you can always stop using them and go back to business as usual anytime. Or, you can adjust them to fit you after you've tried what I suggest.

Extreme Self-Care

Attaining and maintaining a positive attitude, even with all of the best tools, suggestions, and support, can be tough business. I know from experience you're going to need some serious reinforcements in the form of extreme self-care. Self-care is taking the time, every day, to do those things that buoy your spirit and fill your cup. The great thing about effective self-care is that it is all about you.

Extreme self-care is where you put yourself first on the list and stop caring for others before yourself. For the foreseeable future, you're going to the head of the class—a class of *one*.

A little-known fact about me is that I am an introvert. I get my energy from spending time alone.

If I don't practice good self-care with alone time, eventually I turn into a cranky-pants-wearing, ornery person. Most of the time, I am an optimistic, positive-attitude-having, finder of goodness. My self-care practices of meditation, exercise, journaling, visualization, pedicures, facials, and regular massages all contribute to my overall well-being and happiness. You'll note that my self-care practices are mostly solo activities. I don't have to, nor do I want to, do them with another person, and that's precisely the point.

If you are an introvert, you'll want to identify solo activities that keep your energy stores high.

Extroverts, on the other hand, recharge by being around people. Left alone too long, they can sink into a moderate depression. This is particularly important to note when you are post-divorce and in the depression stage of the grief process.

It is hard to go against our innate nature, so you must identify yourself as an introvert or an extrovert, and choose your extreme self-care practices accordingly. For instance, your exercise may consist of group classes. You may always want to get a pedicure with a friend. I'm perfectly content to stay home and watch a movie on the couch, while my husband would much prefer to be out in the world around people.

How you're wired is how you're wired, and there is nothing wrong with you. The trick is to identify your basic settings and honor them with extreme self-care activities that recharge your spirit.

If you're unsure about whether you are an introvert or an extrovert (or even a combination of the two, known as an ambivert), you'll want to check out the book, *Quiet: The Power of Introverts in a World That Can't Stop Talking* by Susan Cain.

I suspect that very soon after you begin to engage in extreme self-care activities, you will start to feel more like yourself again. Actually, you'll feel better than your old self, and in fact, become inspired to really take your new life by the horns.

Moving On:
Your Action Steps for Moving Forward

✓ Stop any Mental Malpractice you might be engaged in, and instead ...

✓ Start using the Mental Ninja Tricks.

✓ BOLO! Make a list of what you're looking out for, and check them off when you find or see them.

✓ Practice Extreme Self-Care. You deserve the best.

Chapter Four:
Find Your Tribe and Build Your Bench

Friends are the family we choose for ourselves. —Edna Buchanan

As your life has changed from the very act of getting divorced, other aspects of your life have changed as well. The key players in your life may be drastically different. This change may have come as a surprise. Or maybe you've been divorced long enough by now it isn't surprising to understand that when you lost a spouse, you also lost family and friends. As you've gone from having a husband or a wife, so have you gone from having, to not having, in-laws, including a mother in-law, father in-law, possibly brothers and sisters in-law, nieces and nephews, and maybe even cousins and grandparents in-law. That's a lot of change! Everyone is now referred to as "former," and these changes can be almost as disconcerting as the divorce itself.

You might have had couples friends, people with whom you shared dinners, celebrations, and maybe even holidays. The structure and function of your family has changed, either dramatically or slightly, as have some (or all) of your friends.

The saying "blood is thicker than water" might never be more accurate than during a divorce. While people who previously treated you as though you were naturally born into their family may now treat you politely, most people will feel loyal to the person to whom they are related. They might like you just fine, and if your divorce wasn't too nasty, they may not mind keeping a civil, good, or even close relationship with you. But I've heard more often than not that people find it easier to keep their original allegiances and either maintain their distance or cut ties altogether from nonfamily members after divorce.

When it comes to friendships, the friends you brought into the relationship are most likely the friends you'll take with you when you leave. Notwithstanding any marital issues your best friend might be having, or fears they possess about their own marriage ending in divorce, your best friend will stay your best friend. Your parents, siblings, and grandparents, in most cases, will support you.

Voila, There's a Void

What you might find is that you feel a void left by former relatives and friends. You might have noticed that your divorce has caused some people to disconnect, lose touch, or avoid you. On the flip side, you might have noticed something else that's actually pretty cool: Some people will seek you out because they've been there, done that, and they know a little something about what you might need right about now.

In addition to a "changing of the guard" as it were, it's not uncommon to retreat into oneself after divorce. You've either noticed a huge change or lost significant relationships you previously viewed as life-long. A natural reaction is to withdraw not only from those relationships, but also from developing new ones. Part of establishing a friendship is the sharing of oneself, and new friendships require a special brand of sharing. You have to let a new person get to know you and vice versa. Maybe not everything needs to be shared all at once, but it's good to open up at least a little, and that means you have to step out of your shell, which may feel counterintuitive, and extend yourself to someone you don't already know and trust. This might be one of the hardest parts of post-divorce life you will have to contend with.

This chapter may have caused you to stop and reflect on the state of some of your relationships, and if so, I wouldn't be surprised. If you're sad or even a little bummed out about the state of some of your long-held relationships and the prospects of future ones, you're not alone. I divorced a military man, and therefore, I also divorced the military. One day I was a spouse who was friends with the other spouses, invited to events, kept in the know, and even had commissary privileges. The next day, I was *persona non grata*. One day I was in the club, and the next day I was out. I absolutely understand how disconcerting it can be to experience a change in the people you've assumed would always be there.

I want to weigh in and say something positive (I know, shocking right?): Your situation and prospects for the future are better than you can possibly imagine! You get to intentionally and purposefully fill the void. It will be easier than you think, and the sooner you get started, the sooner you're going to get the results (new friendships and more!) you desire.

Yes, that's right. You can find new members of your tribe, including friends and associates, and build your bench of support and encouragement, in both friendship and in love. In chapter 7, I'm going to talk about the process of finding new love and everything that can, and will, go along with it. Almost always, a new love comes fully stocked with a new bunch of other people (they could even become your new in-laws). I know, I'm getting ahead of myself just a little. Now, I want to talk about building your bench.

In business coaching, I encourage my clients to build their bench. They need to identify mutually beneficial relationships, and I believe you need a strong personal bench, too. These relationships are with folks who have similar values, beliefs and goals, are complementary in nature, and offer the support you need. You can't have too many of them, and there's no time like the present to begin your search.

You may call some very special people lifetime friends, and they've stuck around and weathered the divorce storm with you. You might have already attracted some wonderful new people into your life, even if just by chance.

On the flip side, maybe your circumstances have left you without even one person you'd call a close friend. Whether you're feeling pretty good about your current social status, or ready to paint a new masterpiece on your fresh canvas, I'm not going to make you guess about the best way to find new friends and make new connections. I'm going to point you in the right direction. You've probably guessed by now that I'm not really a leave it to chance kind of gal.

The secret of attraction is to love yourself. Attractive people judge neither themselves nor others. They are open to gestures of love. They think about love, and express their love in every action. —Deepak Chopra

Having Your Groove Is Attractive

In order to attract fantastic new relationships into your life, there is one person to whom you must become irresistible. *Yourself.* When you are authentically attractive to yourself, seeing yourself as likable and lovable, then *and only then* will you release the pheromones that will make you attractive to others. I'm not speaking about romantic relationships right now at all (although a healthy self-esteem and self-confidence tend to attract prospective romantically-interested folks in droves). The truth is this: Self-confidence and authenticity are the foundational elements of "having your groove" and your overall attractiveness. Being comfortable in your own skin allows others to be comfortable with themselves around you. You won't feel the need to impress others and will experience a shift by naturally attracting people who value you and the genuine relationship they are honored to have with you.

You might have thought I was going to, right off the bat, give you the 1-2-3 of the when, where and how to find new friends ... and I'm going to. But the very first step is actually to turn the focus solely on you. The truth is the journey to these wonderful new relationships starts with you getting your groove back.

So, Let's Get Your Groove Back!

If you've done any of the previously suggested work in this book, or you've been divorced for awhile, you might already have some of your old swagger back, and that's terrific. The further you get from your date of divorce, and the closer you get to your two-year divorce-i-versary, the better and better you are predestined to feel. In addition, the more you focus and work on yourself, the better and better you'll feel. But just in case you would like to feel better faster (and for some of you, feel good at all), there are a few things you can do right away:

1. Read one of my favorite books, *The Miracle Morning.* Suffice it to say I wish I'd had this book as I was going through my divorce. The minute I found the book, I realized two things: One, I was already doing each of the practices, and the book was validation of their efficacy. Two, practicing the *Life S.A.V.E.R.S.* on a consistent basis is the shortest, fastest, easiest, and most effective way through a divorce (whether the divorce is "easy" or tumultuous in nature). The *Life S.A.V.E.R.S* are silence, affirmations, visualization, exercise, reading, and scribing. The book goes into great detail about how to effectively use these six practices to set yourself up for an amazing day. When implemented daily, you'll soon find yourself living an amazing life. And speaking of building your bench, there's a robust community on Facebook where you can find lots of amazingly positive people who practice the *Life S.A.V.E.R.S.* and would be thrilled to support you (a.k.a. new friends). You can join The Miracle Morning™ Community on Facebook by simply doing a search and requesting to join.

2. Get into the gym. While the *E* for exercise is included in the *Life S.A.V.E.R.S.* (and I'm going to assume you're reading this book to find out more), it deserves special attention here. Breaking a sweat, feeling your blood pumping through your veins, getting in shape, or even wearing that pair of pants you haven't worn since college will make you feel better on multiple levels. You'll improve your overall health, stamina, energy, and optimism and decrease your stress, anxiety, and depression (and quite possibly, your pant size, too)!

3. Be sociable. Finding new friends is a little like dating. At the risk of becoming Captain Obvious for a minute, I have to state what you probably already know: If you don't get out and meet new people, you'll miss out on the benefits of surrounding yourself with like-minded people who can understand and support you. I promise you there is someone who is walking the same path and would love to not only commiserate, but also strategize with you. Another person who has been there, done that can offer wisdom and insight that can come in handy at crucial times.

One of the challenges with divorce is that to do it well, your best option is to have already done it well. Except that, if you're reading this book, you've most likely experienced your first divorce. One of the sayings of the online support site DivorceForce.com is "If I knew then what I know now." It's tough to gain experience without actually going through an experience. The next best thing is a friend, or group of friends, who has already made it through, or who is a little further down the path than you are right now.

Decide that you're going to be willing to open up (okay, maybe just a little for the time being), and get out into the world.

- Take a class in something you already enjoy doing, such as cooking, painting, or learning a language.

- Go back to school. Maybe a career change is in order. Do you need a degree or certification? You're always young enough to enroll in a class or change your career, but you're as old as you've ever been today, and you're never going to be younger than you are now. (In other words: don't let age or years stand in your way; it is simply no excuse, and there's no time like the present to get started.)

- If it's been a while since you've been to church and church is your thing, *go*. If you don't have one already, it might take a minute to find a new church home. Feel free to try a few on for size until you find one that fits, and then get involved.

- If church isn't your thing, perhaps a Tony Robbins or other personal development seminar will do the trick. There's nothing like a divorce to set some personal growth in motion, and I'm living proof that a divorce plus some serious personal development (and some intense counseling) can spark a transformation that others will not see coming.

You can find many ways to meet people and develop friendships. You just need to get out and do it.

Not All of Your New Friends Need to be Divorced

If your new friends aren't divorced, chances are they won't understand entirely why you are prone to mood swings, disappearing for a day or two, or still feeling the residual effects of your transition.

And, that's entirely okay. I suggest you develop friends who have never been married and are happily married, as well as those who have been through a divorce.

While it's terrific to have friends who understand your plight, I also need to throw in a few words of caution here. If all you ever talk about with your new friends is your divorce, you are quite possibly doing the exact opposite of what this book is intended to do: focus you firmly on the future. So while it is wise to seek counsel from an experienced ally, you can't fully move forward unless and until you genuinely and intentionally create a new life for yourself, and that includes not only new people and experiences, but also the things that will eventually become the great memories you look back on.

To Have a Friend, Be a Friend

Developing friendships as an adult, a newly divorced and partially wounded, yet highly optimistic adult, can be challenging. I've shared tips to help you find new people, but what do you do with them once you've found them? How do you pursue the ones that seem like a fit initially or let go of the ones that don't?

All good questions, don't you think? I'll do my best to answer them for you. *Smile.*

In my book, *Vision to Reality*, I speak about my concept of relationships called the PLUs or *people like us*. I have a belief that in life you are able to be your best self when you're surrounded by your people, aka PLUs.

Some people will like you. Some people won't like you. *That is okay.* Some people will be your people, and you will resonate with them from the first minute you meet. To find as many of your PLUs as possible, you have to sort and keep sorting because you will probably meet a dozen or even a hundred who aren't PLUs for the one that you do.

If you have or have found a strong post-divorce network of individuals who cheer you on in your pursuit of goals and designing your new life, good for you! But most of the people I've spoken to shared they were seeking, and hungry for, new, deep connections after their divorce. So, you'll just go round up some new friends, right? As luck would have it, it doesn't seem to be that easy.

Statistics show that as we get older, we tend to have fewer close friendships. And, as you've no doubt noticed, not all relationships are guaranteed to last. Unlike when we were in school, attending a summer camp, or seeing kids around the neighborhood, we can't easily use the power of forced consistency to find prospective friends. Every friendship goes through some of, if not all, of the stages: 'I don't know, like, or trust you,' to a place where it feels like you've found a true friend (but not every friendship goes that far, or lasts). So, you've got to know what to do and then do it with a little bit of expectation on the side.

It might be an important note that even though as adults we *have* fewer friends, that doesn't mean we don't *want* more friends. It is easy to make the assumption that the people we want to befriend already have all of the close relationships they want, and in my research, I've found that's not necessarily true.

In order to make new friends, there are a few easy steps you most likely already know and have used many times before. See if these seem logical to you:

Decide. Yup, step numero uno is to decide you want new friends. Next, you'll identify someone who seems like they could be a PLU, and remember ...

To have a friend, you must be a friend. Said another way, do unto others as you would have others do unto you. Your PLUs are going to want the same things in a friendship, give or take a few slight differences, you do. So if you would like someone to remember your birthday, treat you to lunch, invite you over for some French pressed coffee, or encourage you to achieve your goals, then *do that for someone else*. Sounds easy, right? Show up and do for the person or persons you want to be friends with what you would like them to (eventually) do for you. Speaking of showing up ...

Be consistent. In our instant coffee and microwave popcorn world, it is easy to want and expect, instant gratification. But deep, true relationships take time to develop. While you might hit it off with someone right away, decide you were separated at birth, and declare each other to be your new bestie or best buddy, remember this: The best and deepest relationships are built over time. The more you hang out, listen, create fun memories, and even show loyalty and strength during the tough times, the deeper the relationship will be. So let it take the time it takes. Okay? And, while you're out searching for your new friends, always ...

Be friendly. Seems like a simple, common sense piece of advice right there, doesn't it? I know I'm not talking about you, but I have run into some people who are not friendly. If you "don't like people," or consider yourself shy or introverted in nature, you won't always come across as friendly, and being friendly is kind of the number one way anyone is going to know you would make a good friend. Turn up your friendly, friend, so you won't miss out on a friendship that might otherwise have been perfect for you! Oh, and remember to ...

Be quiet. I suggest that you zip it, or keep whatever someone tells you to yourself, whether you think it's confidential, a secret, or private ... or not. If someone tells me something, I assume it's not to be shared, unless they tell me otherwise or I clarify by asking specifically. Yes, there are things I say to my close friends I would not otherwise utter out loud to others, because I want their confirmation, opinion, help, or something else. Your close friends can do the same for you, and will expect the same from you.

See, I told you making friends was about being a good friend, and you've got this. None of the above points are difficult, right?

Be Authentic

If you spent years with your former spouse as your best, closest and/or only friend, keep this in mind as you're making new friends:

You can't do the wrong thing with the right person, and you can't do the right thing with the wrong person.

In other words, if someone is going to like you, they are going to like you. And if they aren't, they aren't (and there's not a lot you can do about it). Your best bet is to be your authentic self, which ironically is easier than altering your personality and will more easily attract others to you (and you'll like yourself a whole lot more, too). This applies to friendships, and it also applies to relationships (more on those in Chapter 7).

What this revelation means for you is that if you are your authentic, wonderful self, you will find friends and supporters who will think you're just great. The discovery that being yourself is a great thing means you can start being yourself right now. You can be genuine every day from this day forward, in every situation, including during your dates, and right into any relationship that might pop up, without the fear that the right person is going to reject you. The right person will be delighted they've found you, and everyone else will self-select out.

It means that you can have a busy career, friends you see on a regular basis, a religion you practice passionately, twelve kids, sixteen horses and seventy-two dogs, and there will be someone who will think that's *just great*.

Living from a place of authenticity allows you to be yourself from the first minute, conserving energy by leaving out the first few months (or years) of showing up as your "representative." You can call and ask someone to lunch, be available last minute, return calls, send "thinking of you" texts, and the person you're developing a relationship with will think whatever you do is *just great*. Who you truly are will be so attractive to the right people they won't be able to help wanting to hang out with you!

You don't have to play by the rules because, with the right people, the only rules are your rules and their rules. And, those rules will be nicely in sync, thank you very much.

In case the idea of being more authentic leaves you needing more information, here are my guidelines for fully engaging in this process:

First, trust yourself. You know when something feels right and when it doesn't. Allow yourself to be fully yourself and to notice how those around you respond. If they don't like you in your full you-ness, they aren't the right people for you to have in your life.

Second, trust the process. If this attempt is your first go at being authentic and attracting what you want, you may fall back into those old behaviors of yore, the ones that don't work. Relax. Breathe. Remind yourself why you're doing what you're doing. You can't do the wrong thing with the right person.

Just like a good diet and exercise program, this new, proactive approach on your being-ness and behavior takes a while for the results to kick in. You don't eat steamed broccoli and grilled chicken for three days and expect to hit your goal weight, unless your goal was to lose about half a pound. So sit back, relax, and know that you're on the right path and that sooner or later the path will get you where you want to go.

Third, enjoy everything that happens as it happens. When you are authentic, you are relaxed. You are happy. You are joyful. You are able to allow, and you are able to enjoy what's happening. You aren't wondering, *Is this person* *going to be my new best friend?* And you will certainly not put any undue pressure or expectation in or on to any conversation or event. Your best bet is to enjoy each person as you meet them. When you let go of what's going to happen next, you can fully enjoy right now. So, get busy enjoying right now, and someday you'll look back, realize you've been friends for a decade, and wonder where the time went.

Remember this: The person (*you*) who is truly enjoying life is irresistibly attractive to anyone and everyone. You will get all kinds of interest from all kinds of people. Just you wait and see!

What's Next?

You now have the where to go and what to do under control, but there's a final bit of work for you to do before you don your finest and roll out the door.

A quick, yet important, analysis of the gaps in your friendships can help you determine what it is you need next and what you need most out of your friendships and relationships.

Take a look at your closest friendships, relationships, and other connections and ask yourself some of these revealing questions:

1. What are the qualities and characteristics I need in a close relationship? For example, integrity, positive, cheerful, focused, successful, supportive, etc.

2. Who do I need to let go of or keep at a distance?

3. Who do I know I need to know better? What kinds of people do I need to get to know better?

4. Who specifically (people you know or types of people) would be the best addition to my bench?

I hope by now you feel confident you can embrace your new life and go out into the world armed with everything you need to find some amazing new friendships.

The right friends can add incredible richness to life, and I wish that you find just the right people (and soon)!

Moving On:
Your Action Steps for Moving Forward

✓　Do what you need to do to get your groove back.

✓　Identify the type of support system you would like to have, and put one in place.

✓　Make some new friends. The right friends are awesome.

Chapter Five: Becoming Everything You Were Meant to Be - Turn Your Pain into Your Vision and Plan

Success is having the courage, the determination, and the will to become all you believe you were meant to be. —George Sheehan

This book is all about how to turn the end of your marriage and pain of your divorce into a life you truly love. Now, I'm not here to suggest that you could not have become all you were meant to be within your marriage. I know for me the life I live today simply wouldn't have been possible if I were still in my first marriage—for a multitude of reasons. What I also know, for a fact, is that the end of a significant relationship can be an unparalleled catalyst to a delightful new beginning.

Every divorced person I've ever spoken to has shared with me that their life is very different, and most of the time and in many ways much better than, what it was before.

There doesn't seem to be a prevailing message from the world-at-large that the end of a marriage is anything other than the end of a marriage. I did not receive even a hint that, once I completed my healing process, there was a better life waiting for me. I heard nothing other than, "I'm sorry to hear that," when I told someone I had gone through a divorce (and their half-hearted apology was usually accompanied by a look of pity). Sometimes, I could feel the other person backing away, as if I had some strain of divorce flu they didn't want to catch.

What would have been more helpful to hear was something like, "I'm sorry to hear you got divorced. In case no one has told you, the best is yet to come." Had any of my previously divorced brothers or sisters shared even a glimmer of hope of the bright future I could create, I might have embraced the healing process sooner and engaged in my transformation even faster. I mean, what is the point of going through the pain of the healing process if you're not expecting something great to come out of it?

If reading this book is the first time you've heard with regards to your divorce, "the best is yet to come!" I'm sorry to hear that. The rest of this book is dedicated to giving you the tools, strategies, and ideas you need to get to the good part as quickly as possible. I wish I had spent less time stuck in the mud, wallowing in my own self-pity, and more time getting over it and getting on with it. So without further ado, let's get on with it for you, shall we?

The plan for reinvention

I'm almost giddy as I write this. You're not only in for a total transformation, you are actually potentially engaging in a complete and total reinvention of yourself and every area of your life. You have the opportunity to, if you so choose, scrutinize every nook and cranny of your life and make adjustments, alterations, or even complete overhauls.

With the clean slate a divorce decree provides, you get to choose every aspect of your new life and your future down to the minutiae. Your finances, your friendships, your physical body, even your work, can all get a very close look. You can examine every facet of yourself, and you can either leave them as is or you can take them down to the studs, as they say, and rebuild from scratch.

Just because you have the opportunity to change something, doesn't always mean you should. And if you decide that you want to throw out all of your belongings, disconnect from every one of your friends, quit your job, and run away from home, you can! You don't have to do all of them in the same day, however.

Even if every area of your life needs immediate attention, or so you think, they don't all need all of your attention at once. You can take one area of your life at a time, one step at a time, one day at a time. It is easy to throw the baby out with the bathwater, especially if you feel as though you have long suppressed desires or have been unable to fully express yourself for what seems like forever. Keep in mind, my friend, that you have the whole rest of your life. Take a deep breath, and let's do the first things first.

Make a list, and check it twice ... a day.

If you are like I was after my divorce, you realized there was a whole list of things you had wanted to do, places you have always wanted to go, and experiences you had been anxious to try, but for one reason or another you've put them off—many of them for years. Perhaps your spouse just wasn't into them or there wasn't the money to do them. You probably had a host of other reasons why you didn't pursue your passions and interests. That is why you need to write down what you truly want. You don't want them to fall prey to those reasons in your new life.

If you don't have a journal yet, I recommend that you get one (I personally use and love the Bullet Journal. You can find out all about it at bulletjournal.com).

In your journal, you will want to create is a list of all of those things to do, places to go, and delicious experiences to have. Part of what you get to do next is check things off of that list! You can, right away, get busy trying, tasting, experimenting, and going anywhere and everywhere you want. In other words, you can start living your life *and there's no better time than the present!*

I do want to note that while there may be many things on your wish list, all of them might not be doable at the moment. You might feel scared to try new things, you might self-sabotage due to an upper-limit challenge, or perhaps you just can't put something in the budget right now. That's quite okay! I want you to keep in mind that as you put one foot in front of the other, and try new things, you'll build "try new things" muscles and even save money over time. Be gentle on yourself, and take it one step at a time.

My recommendation is you stop right here and start a list. I'll wait ...

Did you finish your list? If so, congratulations! Except I would be remiss if I didn't casually mention that this list is a living document. What that means is, even as you cross off one or two things, you're probably going to add three or even 10 more things. Once you learn French, you probably want to go live in France for a month. You'll realize that Spanish and Italian are very close because they are all Romance languages and probably want learn them, too. This will mean you also need to live in Spain and Italy for a time. As you get into the best shape of your life, you realize your wardrobe needs a complete overhaul. You'll want to replace every item in your closet, which will also require new accessories. Either you've moved into a new home, or you have the same home you used to share with your former spouse. You will probably want to get new bedroom furniture, if you haven't already, and redecorating one room quite possibly will give you the bug to redo all the rest of them.

I'm sure you can see where I'm going with this. Just as your list will continue to grow and evolve, so will you. Your transformation is a never-ending odyssey.

Make Art

You might be tempted to skip over this section, especially if you've been ignoring your creative side in favor of a fast-paced career in the corporate world or general life busy-ness for the past decade (or more). Please don't.

In case you are thinking, "I'm not creative" (I used to think this, too), there's no actual definition of being creative. If you're doing something that makes your soul happy, you're probably being creative. Whatever you're doing, know this: creative people are actually happier than noncreative people, that is people who are failing to create.

The benefits of doing something creative, whether you consider yourself artistic or not, have been heavily documented. So I won't speak to the scientific or technical reasons why you should unleash your creative side as one element of your transformation. I'm simply going to suggest that you begin a creativity practice and very soon (the sooner the better). Creativity, creating art, has an unlimited number of forms. Baking, writing, sculpting, painting ... These are just a few of the ways you can express your creativity. You can find classes or groups to help you unleash your artistic side.

How do I know? Well, you're reading my art right now. I didn't grow up wanting to be an author; writing never even crossed my mind! But after my divorce, as I was growing my coaching and speaking business, Mark Victor Hansen (you'll know him as the co-author of the *Chicken Soup for the Soul* book series) told me to take my most popular speech and turn it into a book. So I did. What happened next is nothing short of remarkable—I discovered that I liked writing, seemed to be okay at it, and even have a knack for it. I started blogging, created a weekly newsletter, and realized I really enjoyed it. The book you hold in your hands is my nineteenth book. You might say I took my creativity and ran with it. My spirit is happier and all the better for it. So is my bank account.

I'm not suggesting that you need to turn your art into a business or an income stream of any kind. It may simply be an outlet for you, a hobby that makes you happy. It isn't *what* you do, it's *that* you do something. It's your art, and how it looks or turns out doesn't even matter. But you're going to use your art to get back in the groove, identify your new groove really, in a way that feeds your soul.

Even if you consider yourself the least creative person on earth (a title I previously held myself), your spirit doesn't know that. It seeks expression in its own special way, and will reward you for giving it the attention it deserves.

The sooner you indulge in a creative practice, the faster you'll feel more like yourself. By yourself, I mean your new post-divorce, happily transformed self.

Your Work

Perhaps a piece of your transformation calls for a new career or a strong adjustment in the career you have now. You might want to work with a career coach to determine what you really want to do with the rest of your life. We'll talk more about that in an upcoming chapter.

Your Friendships

During the course of your transformation, you are bound to attract some new and exciting friends and more-than-friends into your life (especially if you follow my advice from the previous chapter). And, you're going to let more people go than just your spouse.

Your Hobbies

Many doses of newfound joy, and even some of your best new relationships, will be the fruit of the hobby trees you grow. And, yes, you guessed it: more on that in an upcoming chapter.

So, what will your new life look like? You may want a new career, a new set of friends, and the chance to explore new passions. We'll explore how to approach all of these in upcoming chapters, but first we have to discover what you have in mind for your new future, especially if you haven't had a chance to take stock and define a new vision. Out of that new vision will spring how you spend your day-to-day life and with whom.

Your New Life Plan

Along with your lists of things to do and the art you're creating, the time has come to carefully craft a new plan for your life. In the remainder of this chapter, I'm going to start you on the journey of defining your vision and your purpose. In the next chapter, we'll tackle goal setting and writing out your full new plan.

Once upon a time, you had a plan that included a vision that included your former spouse. You presumably envisioned growing old together and the many adventures you would have along the way. Your life had purpose, and you set goals based on your vision and took action on the plan that supported that vision.

If you're like some of the people I interviewed for this book, you spent decades together and *had* many of those adventures. Or perhaps you spent only a few years together and abruptly found yourself having to write a new vision, and it seems too soon.

I promise you, the further you get from the date of your divorce, the more those feelings will dull, and you'll find yourself eager to lean into and enjoy your new life.

Whether you're more than ready to dive in to your next phase or you're reading this with great reluctance, the truth is this: now you have the opportunity to design and define a new life plan for yourself. You have a clean canvas, and you are the exclusive artist on this very important art project.

Left to chance, your life will happen to you instead of emanating from you. Take the time to intentionally design the rest of your life with thoughtful purpose and you will love it so much more than if you sit passively on the sideline.

If you and I are on the same page and what you want is to live an amazing life so you can enjoy every moment, live your dreams, and perhaps find new and wonderful relationships, let's create a vision that will change the course of your life. Before you can begin your new life, you absolutely must have one heck of a fierce life-long vision.

Are you ready? Let's begin!

Your Vision

Vision is what you see in your mind's eye, not something you see externally. You don't leave on vacation without knowing your destination, and this new life-after-divorce journey is no different.

If you've never created a true vision before, it may seem like an exercise that is vague and intangible. However, I can assure you that the long-term benefits are substantial and will help you create simply amazing results. Your vision, once crystalized, will pull you forward. It will get you up early and keep you up late. It will excite you, even when you experience the inevitable challenges that are bound to show up: you get off-track, sick, or you hit a roadblock or two. Indeed, your vision is the glue that holds your whole life together in the best of times, as well as in the toughest of times.

What is a Vision?

Your vision is your "what." When you close your eyes and think of what you truly want, you'll find that a picture of those desires appears on the mental screen of your mind. I encourage you to envision something long-term, such as ten or even twenty years (or longer) in the future. What's the ultimate vision you're working toward? Is it the completion of a new degree, buying and eventually selling a business, raising your children to be amazing, happy adults, or finding new love? There are no right or wrong answers; aim for what your heart desires. Write down five things you want to have accomplished ten years or more in the future. Here are some ideas to get you started:

- Find and buy a business that produces enough income to support me and build significant wealth.

- Complete my first Ironman triathlon (marathon, 10K, etc.).

- Be happily, joyfully remarried to my best friend.

- Build new and supportive friendships.

- Complete my recovery.

- Explore my spirituality and identify practices and beliefs that work for me.

- Own my own home outright.

- Payoff my car, debt, home, student loans, etc.

- Create a leveraged stream of income in excess of $10,000 per month.

If you're having trouble getting started, you may not be convinced of the power of creating a vision. You also might not believe that you can create a new vision or that creating one will bring it into being, especially if your previous vision never quite came to pass. I understand, I really do.

I'll take that as a challenge and do my best to convert you to a bona fide enthusiastic vision-creator. Here are just a few reasons why visioning is something you should do:

- Visioning breaks you out of boundary thinking. As you open your mind and your mind's eye to new possibilities, you will begin to shed previous limitations. With the right questions, you will begin to imagine the "what ifs" and with time, you will come to understand that they are not out of reach.

- Visioning provides continuity of thinking and action and helps you avoid the stutter effect of planning fits and starts. Having a defined, clear vision that is reviewed and visualized often—in other words, multiple times daily—will help you avoid "New Year's Eve syndrome," where goals are set and then forgotten in about two weeks (until the next New Year).

• Your vision automatically identifies your future direction and purpose. It grabs hold of your interest, strengthens your commitment, and promotes laser-like focus. When you have a clear picture in your mind of where you're going, it is always there, accessible and readily available to pull you in the right direction. Having a clear mental picture you can immediately access is especially helpful when fears and doubts creep in.

• Visioning encourages openness to unique and creative solutions. As you hold your clearly defined vision, the ways to make that vision present itself Your subconscious mind works on your behalf to spot opportunities, prospects, and possibilities you might otherwise have missed.

• Visioning promotes and builds confidence. Have you ever noticed how a person who has a purpose and a vision carries himself or herself in a certain way? They are positive, upbeat, and yes, confident. When you create your vision, your confidence will be magnetic and will attract that clearly defined future reality attracting your clearly defined vision to you. It is likely your self-confidence took a hit during your divorce, and having a new vision will restore and even enhance it.

Are you convinced?

You already have created in your life what you previously held as a vision, even if you didn't realize that's what you were doing. In other words, each person usually has a vision they hold in mind, even if they don't capture it in writing or express it out loud. This time, if you didn't do it before, you're creating it on purpose and with purpose. And I promise it will serve you well.

Think of visioning as bringing thoughts to fruition, only this time you're directing your imagination to create your future one magical moment at a time. Do you agree with me that now is the time to use your subconscious mind, through the use of this picturing tool called visioning, to create what you truly desire? Okay, then, let's do this!

Your Visioning Exercise

I suggest you set aside an entire morning, or a block of 2-4 hours, to dive into this exercise. Go somewhere you can remain uninterrupted. It is a challenge to get back to where you were after a phone call or other interruption—the last thing you want is to have your flow interrupted.

Start the process of creating your vision by daydreaming. Begin to imagine and create a colorful, clear picture in your mind of what your life, career, home, and relationships will look like with the expectation that energy, people, space, and money are no object.

Next, zero in on the areas of your post-divorce life that need a clearer vision. How can your home environment, friendships, family relationships, physical body, or even career be markedly improved? In short, what areas of your life aren't yet working as well as you would like? Are you as strong, fit, financially sound, balanced, fulfilled, and loved as you wish to be?

From there, create a big, overall vision, including your desired income, the look and feel of your personal relationships, where and how you want to live, travel, and other aspects of life you want to explore. Then, you'll create a unique vision for each of those areas.

Now, describe in vivid detail, in writing, what your ideal day looks like. Include a description of your surroundings (home, office, family, and friends). Open a new file document on your computer, find a journal that speaks to your soul, or use a good old-fashioned yellow legal pad. The choice is yours; do what feels right to you.

When you've captured the essence of what you want, take the exercise one step further by working backward to today from that vision. In other words, if you want to have your ideal day ten years from now, where do you need to be in five years? A year from now? And, my personal favorite, 100 days from now.[1] Ask yourself, "What is my preferred future?"

Keep the following in mind as you work on your vision:

- Draw on your beliefs, mission, and the mental picture of your ideal environment. You can even find inspiration in others you know or know of who have designed a wonderful life after their divorce and perhaps some of the stories in this book.

- Describe in detail what you want to see in your life and in the future.

- Be specific to each area of your life. Start with the big picture, and drill down to the nitty gritty if you'd like.

- Be sure to remain positive and inspired. Sometimes the distance between where you are today and where you want to be seems too great, and I promise you it is not! You will get there, one day, action, and step at a time.

- Be open to a massive upgrade, lots of changes, and a really big leap! *The best is yet to come.*

Here are some questions to get you started creating your vision:

- In your preferred future, what time does your day start? End? How many hours do you work and spend on your hobbies or with your family. How is your day structured?

- Who is with you? Your success is determined in large part by the people you surround yourself with, and it is time to become clear about whom you want to attract into your life in the future.

- What activities do you want included in your days, weeks, months, and years?

- What type of work are you doing, and with whom? Describe the types of partners, co-workers, employees, clients and customers you have. Describe the relationships you have with those on your team. Synergistic relationships begin first in your mind.

- Where is your office located? Do you have multiple locations? Do you work at home, in an office, or in both places? Be sure to include the type of supplies or equipment you work with, all those neat furnishings, plants, pictures, etc.

- If you have business partners, sales people, investors, employees, how many do you have, and what are they like?

- What is your ideal living space? Where is it located? How is it decorated? Who is there to greet you at the end of your day?

- What do you drive? How does it make you feel?

- Where do you vacation? With whom? How often?

- If you have children, write about the type of parent you are, how you want your children to feel about you, and about your relationship as a whole.

- Who are your friends? What other significant relationships do you have?

Extra thought-provoking and helpful questions:

- What will you gain from achieving your vision?

- What will the world gain from you achieving your vision?

- Who is going to help you?

- Who is going to help you enjoy the rewards?

- Where will you work on your vision?

- Where will you celebrate its achievement? How often will you take the time to celebrate? How will you celebrate your progress and achievements?

- When do you want to achieve different aspects of your vision?

- When will you start working on your vision?

- Why on earth are you going to dedicate your time, talents, and resources to work toward this vision?

- Why must you achieve your vision?

- Why are you worth your vision? I think that you deserve it because you're alive, but dive into why you deserve to achieve it *now*.

Brainstorm. Be specific. Be playful. Be creative. Make the vision of your life the way you want it. After all, it's your life and your vision.

Note: It is important to put your vision in writing. There is power in the written word. Just the act of writing down what you want sets the creative process in motion. Give yourself enough uninterrupted, focused time to go from start to finish of your first draft. Again, I recommend blocking out at least two hours to complete the questions above. Then, let your vision sit for a while (a week, maybe two?) and come back to it after you've had time to reflect. Your vision is alive and will constantly evolve. Keep in mind that what you think you want may actually not be what comes to fruition, but what comes to fruition may actually be better!

Vision Killers

As you engage in the visioning process, you may encounter obstacles that also happen to be people. Your ex, in-laws, or even people you thought were once your best friends might have a thing or two to say about what you have planned in the future.

Just because you are on board with designing and creating your new destiny doesn't mean everyone around you will be ... or even can be. Be alert to the fact that you may encounter the following vision killers, and be ready to ignore them.

Here are a few to look out for, and when you spot them, smile to yourself and keep going.

Tradition: Be careful of the phrase "But you've always done it this way." Know that your new life is not bound by the limitations of your old one.

Fear of ridicule: You may come across people who meet your new aspirations with derision. Most often the people who criticize are those who have neglected to create their own vision and who come from a place of fear instead of power. Have compassion for them, but don't listen to them. My mantra is: *If I want your opinion, I'll give it to you.* You're welcome to use mine, or craft one of your own.

Stereotypes of people, conditions, roles, and outcomes: You may hear, "Why do you think you can achieve this?" Your answer: "Why not me?" Don't be surprised if some people in your life can see you as capable of doing or achieving only certain things. Let them keep those limitations for themselves. You owe it to yourself to go for what you really want.

Naysayers: Very simply, refuse to listen to anyone who doesn't absolutely, 100 percent support your vision, no matter who they are. Period.

Look, some of these folks are wanting to help you and warn you against doing something that could cause you to get hurt or make you lose everything. Most likely, they are coming from a good place and don't mean to inflict the harm that comes from sowing seeds of "you can't succeed." Their advice and intention are run through their own filters, and those filters are often chock-full of limiting beliefs, past failures, and even frustration with their own lack of success.

Should you need words of encouragement, I believe these from Will Smith in the movie *Pursuit of Happyness,* will do the trick:

> *Don't ever let somebody tell you...*
> *...you can't do something.*
> *Not even me.*
> *- All right? - All right.*
> *You got a dream...*
> *...you gotta protect it.*
> *People can't do something themselves...*
> *...they wanna tell you you can't do it.*
> *If you want something, go get it. Period.*

Remember: there is no right or wrong way to write or fulfill your vision. You should describe in complete detail exactly what you, and you alone, desire. It may take up to 20 pages or more, or it may be as simple as one page using bullet points.

Your Purpose: The *Why* Behind the *What*

Knowing what you want is one thing; knowing why you want it is something entirely different. Your vision is what you want; your purpose for getting it is why you want it in the first place. If you want something merely for the sake of wanting it, or because someone told you that you should want it, you probably won't ever get it. Over time what you thought was a strong desire for your outcomes will lessen, or life, post-divorce healing and a myriad of other distractions, will quickly take you off track. If, on the other hand, you know exactly why you want what you want, then you have increased your chances of achievement. By how much? I honestly don't know, but I do know this: *it is a lot.*

The stronger your why, the easier the how becomes. Or in my experience, you won't care how hard it is because you want it badly enough to do whatever it takes to get it. In order to manifest your most ambitious desires, you must know and have a strong emotional connection to *why* you want your *what.*

If some, or all, of your vision is based upon what someone else wants or has wanted, I advise you to ask yourself if it is what you truly want. Now that you're creating your new life, there is no need to hold on to anything that either isn't your original idea or something that doesn't deeply resonate with you today.

I want you to consider letting go of any piece of your vision that isn't accompanied by your strong, burning desire to achieve it. In other words, if are you just filling in the blanks and checking boxes, I have a hunch eventually you will lose steam and your willpower will wane anyway. A sense of clarity about the purpose—the *why*—behind your vision will help it come to you as if by magic. And I have one last important question: What will achieving this vision really give you besides a general sense of accomplishment? What purpose will it serve in your life as a whole?

If your vision is firewood, your purpose is the gas you pour on the wood before you light the fire. The fire burns brighter, hotter, and longer with lots of gas and just the right match to light it up. Your vision will have the fuel it needs when you have a crystal clear purpose.

When you are navigating the different stages of building your new life, you will need a strong, clear vision to keep you going as you encounter the inevitable challenges. Even if you have smooth sailing, and nothing that causes you concern, I promise that the enthusiasm with which you designed your vision will wane, and at some point you will lose your urgency. What that happens, your defined purpose combined with a white-hot internal desire to achieve it, will keep you going.

Your Plan

In my book *Vision to Reality*, I cover how to use a 100-day plan in depth. And as I mentioned just a few pages ago, you can get access to a downloadable version to use.

Just as you have created a clear, long-term vision, it is important to craft an action plan based on that vision. Your plan, or plans as the case may be, will be based on your vision. Depending upon how far in the future you set your vision, you will design plans for relevant time periods using your vision as a reference.

In my case, I work best in five-year increments. Every five years, I design a five-year vision and then create a five-year plan based upon that vision. Next comes a one-year vision and plan and finally, a 100-day plan. Just writing a five-year vision would, without question, get me all excited. But without an action plan to accompany it, you would find me on my couch in a short period of time fully engaged in some sort of Netflix marathon.

Whatever the duration of your vision, it's more than a little important to craft a plan to go along with it. Keep in mind that this is supposed to be *fun*. You're designing your future, for goodness sake, so don't take it too seriously! Stay in your heart, as opposed to getting stuck in your head and writing what you think you're supposed to write. Do what you need to do to thoroughly enjoy the process.

The following elements are key pieces of your plan:

Vision Statement. Take your bigger vision and drill it down to three to five bullet points or sentences that capture its essence. Again, your vision is your *what*.

Purpose Statement. Your purpose statement is your *why* and is as important, if not more important, than the vision statement. Again, just a few sentences will do: Why do you want to achieve this vision? What is it going to do for you, for your life, for those you love, etc.?

Your Top 10 Goals. In the 100-day plan, you will work on just three goals. Because your long-term vision is just that—long-term—you probably have a lot you want to accomplish. A few of those goals you'll tackle right away, some may be predicated upon achieving nearer-term goals, and a few you might want to save for later. Again, remember to keep it fun.

Empowering Descriptors. Your empowering descriptors are keywords you choose to describe yourself, not necessarily yourself of today, but the self of your fully realized vision. These keywords are your reputation to live up to, such as mother of the year, business beast, super stud, gorgeous goddess. You get the idea, right? If you're not chuckling just a little as you write them, and every time you read them, they still need a little work. Got it?

The Eight Areas of Focus. I recommend referring to the well-known, well-used, and well-loved Wheel of Life to help balance your goals and vision across the full spectrum of your life. It includes eight areas of focus to choose from when doing personal and professional development: relaxation and hobbies, mental, emotional, physical, spiritual, family and friends, work, and financial. Depending on how long-term your initial vision is, and especially if it is at least a year to five years in duration, you'll want to identify how you'd like each of these areas to look, feel, and be. You'll notice when you do your initial 100-day plan that I advise you choose only three areas of focus. It should be abundantly clear which three areas need the most focus, not only during your first 100-day plan, but also in each plan that follows.

Resources. I will guide you through putting together your personal success team, otherwise known as the people you have on your bench. In addition to people, you can rely upon other resources to help you achieve your goals, such as other books, seminars, programs, and even music. There's no sense in reinventing the wheel, so identify *what* and *who* you can rely on during your transformation and beyond. You can achieve amazing things, especially if you have guides to show you the way.

Next Steps. This is your "data dump." You're going to get out of your head and on to paper every single action item, to-do item, and task that needs to be done (or at least, right now you think it needs to get done). On this list will go everything from "by mom a birthday card," to "schedule next therapy session" to, "buy a McDonald's franchise." In other words, nothing is too big or too small—if it's rolling around in your head and you need to do it, or you think you do, it goes on this list. Once you have what you consider to be a complete list, start at the top and label each item as a "do, delegate, delay, or dump." You'll do the things that you, and only you can do. If you can delegate something, by all means, delegate it! If it doesn't need to be done within the duration of this particular plan (whether it's one year or five years or 10 years), you get to delay it. Finally, sometimes there are things on our lists that in all actuality and honesty never ever need to really get done. The dump items get erased, or if it makes you feel better, cross them off.

I'd advise you to stop right here and create a plan based on your longer-term vision. Then jump right into the next chapter so that I can guide you through goal setting in a way you may never have seen. Let's set some goals that light you up!

Moving On:
Your Action Steps for Moving Forward

✓   Define your plan for reinvention.

✓   Make your to do, to read, to visit, to see (etc.) list.

✓   Finalize your vision!

---

[1] You can learn more about my 100-day plan in the next chapter and get your own copy by visiting

honoreecorder.com/resources, password *success*. You can read much more about turning your vision to reality in my book, *Vision to Reality*.

Chapter Six:
Goals Get You Up Early and Keep You Up Late

If a goal doesn't challenge you, it won't change you. —Unknown

In *If Divorce is a Game, These are the Rules,* I mentioned goal setting, but didn't discuss it in depth as a practice to help move you forward.

Your transformation won't go into orbit without some powerful goals to propel and pull you forward.

This chapter is your reference for both setting and reaching the goals you've set.

The power of properly set goals is so great, I would be remiss if I didn't do a deep dive for you before you go head-first into creating your first shorter-term (100-day?) plan. Because you are progressing from one major stage of your life (marriage) into a new and different stage, having goals that empower, inspire and keep you going is, dare I say, crucial. I don't want anything to permanently change your course, be too much of an obstacle to overcome, or cause unnecessary delay. Powerful goals are the antidote to these potential problems. So we're going to make a quick stop on Goal Central so you can zoom off to your next great destination. If you follow my suggestions, you can acquire goals that will literally rock your world and change your destiny.

What Setting New Goals Can Do for You

If you've done the exercises in the previous chapter, you've already invested quite a bit of your precious time in designing a new future. Although I've engaged in the practice of visioning for more than two decades, I'm still invigorated by the process every time I do it. Goal setting is no different: It gives me a charge like nothing else, and the charge comes for several reasons:

1. I know I'll have to up my game to achieve the goals I've set.

2. Achieving them means that something amazing will happen, sometimes many amazing things. And, I can't always predict what the amazingness will be (not even close).

3. By reaching my goals, I reinforce my belief in myself, build my self-esteem, and become all I can become day by day.

By creating new goals and acting on the plan that supports them (i.e., designing an environment for success), I purposely keep myself moving forward. But know this: it is impossible to move forward effectively while you're looking in your rearview mirror. Not unlike having your long- and short-term visions, by having goals and focusing on them, you will move forward consistently. The concurrent benefit is that you won't be thinking about the past, which is helpful as you leave your previous marriage in the dust behind you.

Eight More Benefits of Goal Setting

There are even more benefits to taking the time to define some properly set goals, and I'm going to share eight of them with you right now.

Setting meaningful goals can bring:

1. Crystal-Clear Focus. Properly thought-out goals clearly set your intentions and desires and make them easy to hold in your mind.

2. Optimum Use of Resources. It can seem like you don't have enough resources to do everything you want to do, especially if you're in the throes of *Woo-hoo, I'm designing a new life.*

This is fun! I want to do everything! Setting goals can help you to prioritize effectively and allocate your resources for what you really want to do. You won't use up what you have and then wish you'd made another choice later.

3. Effective Use of Time. Of course time is also a resource, but it deserves special attention because it is that important. When you have a goal in mind and two actions you can take you will tend to choose the one that moves you closer to achieving your goal. By applying perspective and priority, you'll be spurred into taking the right action.

4. Peace of Mind. Writing down your goals can help you keep track of all the ideas and to-dos and put them in a mental order that makes sense. You can focus on the task at hand because all that you want to accomplish is in a safe place.

5. Clarity of Decision Making. You will easily remember to ask yourself, "Does this activity get me closer to my goal?" If the answer is yes, you'll do it. If not, you won't hesitate to cross it off of your to-do list (bonus: it feels good to cross something off, right?). You'll know which direction to go when you come to a fork in the road. This ability can be incredibly helpful and lessen the stress you might be feeling.

6. Quick and Easy Measurement of What You Do. Setting SMART goals allows you to measure how effectively you are moving towards achieving them—or not—and make the necessary adjustments.

7. Unlimited Creative Juices and Happy Thoughts. You'll release your most creative juices, in abundance, and have amazingly happy thoughts when you have great goals. And, you'll know where you're going and the steps that will get you there.

8. Effective and Clear Communication with Yourself (and Everyone Else). Goals enable you to communicate what you're going for to other people and enroll them as a part of your support system.

The actual goals you set do not necessarily lead you to happiness by themselves. It's far more likely that who you become on the way to achieving them, including the challenges you overcome, what you learn about yourself, and even the process of figuring out how to get from here to there, is what makes you happy.

From Vision to Reality

Identify your most important goals, and suddenly you're ready to figure out how to make them happen. As if by magic, you can and will develop the attitudes, abilities, skills, resources, connections, and financial capacity to reach them. You will begin seeing previously overlooked opportunities and possibilities. There seems to be a way through to a successful outcome that, before you got really clear, didn't seem navigable. How do you make that happen? I'm delighted you asked!

You must:

- Know what you want,

- Believe it's possible for you, and

- Get moving.

If your bigger vision, purpose, and plan got you excited, crafting clearly defined goals is going to light your fire. Having a crystal clear vision, purpose, and plan, as you may have discovered, makes you want to get into action, get moving, and get things done. Let's set some goals that will intentionally steer your positive and outcome-producing energy in the right direction.

Either You're SMART, or You're Not

I mentioned SMART goals at the start of this chapter. SMART, as it pertains to goal setting, stands for *specific, measurable, attainable, risky,* and *time-sensitive.* SMART goals are the bombdiggity. They eliminate all doubt, inaction, and lack (of time, money, space, people you really like, and so much more). You may have heard this acronym before, and it raises the question: have you really put it to use with regards to your goals? If you haven't, and you probably haven't, chances are you have lots of goals that are actually just hopes, dreams, thoughts, and wishes. You don't want to set just any old goals for your new life after divorce. No, sir, these goals are special because you are on a mission now; you have a vision and a purpose.

And now that you have that vision and purpose, it is time to set some awesome goals based on that white-hot vision you've crafted. Don't waste another minute before you make sure your goals meet the following criteria:

Specific

A specific goal gets achieved. A wishy-washy, "I'm not sure what I want goal" won't be, or at least it's left to chance. It's as simple as that. Refer to your vision and purpose when setting your goals, and all along the way ask yourself some powerful questions. Try these:

- Based on my long-term vision, what do I most want to accomplish?

- What are the most important areas I must focus on with laser-like intensity?

- What is one area where I must make measurable improvement? For example, do I need to make myself smokin' hot, get my emotions in check, live in a more spiritual place, pay off debt or a vehicle, or even make my relationships with my kids magical?

- If my life is going to be a bona fide success, what do I need to accomplish, and how great am I going to feel about it when I do?

If you have a goal of amassing a fortune and achieving global domination, you won't be able to complete all of it right away, but you can put aside a defined dollar amount or percentage of your income over the next month, six months, or year. You can write a few chapters in a book, buy some art for your office, schedule and pay for your next vacation, or set the dates for the next year of marketing events. Even goals such as, *find new love, get married, and have two children* require you to meet new people, go on dates, ask great questions, and sort through what you want and what you don't in a relationship (there tends to be lots of sorting on the way to relationship happiness, I've noticed).

Rest assured you can make progress and gain strong momentum in the very near future.

Measurable

What gets measured and remeasured gets attention. Everything else does not. Therefore, you absolutely must establish concrete criteria for measuring progress, initially and continually, toward the attainment of each and every goal you set.

When you measure your progress, you stay on track, reach or exceed your targeted goals, and experience the exhilaration of achievement that spurs you on to continued effort required to reach your goal. And when you don't, you don't.

To determine if your goal is measurable, ask questions, like these:

- How much? As in, how much money? How much time?
- How many? As in, how many new clients? How many miles or reps? How many dates?
- How will I or anyone else know when the goal has been accomplished?

One mechanism for continual measurement is the Dashboard, which you can download at HonoreeCorder.com/Resources (password *success*). This is a tool I developed for my coaching clients, and I share all about it in *Vision to Reality: How Short Term Massive Action Equals Long Term Maximum Results*, which you might also want to read.

Attainable

I play pretty fast and loose with attainable because my belief is that there's always a way if you're committed. But you have to have a plan, and you have to work that plan as if you're all out of bubble gum and you really, really want bubble gum more than you want life itself.

There are some exceptions: You're a woman, and you want to play for the New Orleans Saints. *No sale.* Best we could get you is ownership. (Now that's a great goal!)

Goals that seemed almost impossible move closer and become attainable, not because your goals shrink, but because you grow and expand to match them. When you list your goals, you build your self-image. You see yourself as worthy of these goals, and you develop the traits and personality that allow you to possess them.

That's why getting clear on what you want and why you're worthy and deserving helps accelerate this process.

Risky

Now wait just a minute, I can almost hear you saying, *what do you mean, "Risky?"*

Risky means that the goal makes you a bit nauseated, or at the very least, incredibly uncomfortable. You know this goal is something you desperately want to achieve, you know it's something that's achievable, and you know it's something achievable by YOU if you put your all into it. However, it will be a risk for you to name it and then do your best to claim it. It's always worth attempting to go after our heart's desires because goals like these tend to make us into the best versions of ourselves. How do you know if you've got the right goals? Thanks for asking. I'm happy to provide the answer:

- If, after you set your goals, you think, *No problem, I've got this*, your goals aren't big enough. Try again.

- If, after you set your goals, you think *There's no way. I'm going to watch some television*, the goal is too big. Try again.

- If, after you set your goals, you think *I'm going to have to give it everything I've*

> *got, but I'm pretty darn sure I can knock this one out of the park with solid, consistent effort; unwavering faith; and a smidge of luck,* then <u>you've got it</u>! You've identified the right-sized goal just for you.

Take the risk, go out on the limb, and lean so far out over it that you think you might fall off. The risk is worth the effort!

Time

Time is simply the duration you've identified that you need to achieve a goal. If you're used my 100-day plan, you've got the "time" part covered; you have until your day 100 to achieve your goals. If you're using a different timeframe, you'll adjust the plan to reflect your ideal period.

I've added another "T" to the process:

Tangible

A goal is tangible when you can experience it with one of the senses: taste, touch, smell, sight, or hearing. When your goal is tangible, or when you tie a tangible goal to an intangible goal, you have a better chance of making it specific and measurable and thus, attainable.

Intangible goals identify the internal changes required to reach more tangible goals. They are the personality characteristics and the behavior patterns you must develop to pave the way to success in your career or for reaching some other long-term goal. Because intangible goals are vital for improving your effectiveness, give close attention to tangible ways for measuring them.

Regular Goal to BHAG!

Now that you know the elements of attainable goals, let's help you set some that will make creating an amazing plan for their achievement easy peasy.

It's goal-setting time: Put pen to paper or fingers to keyboard and write those BHAGs that make you sit straight up in your chair and get all of your cylinders firing. What are BHAGs, you ask? They are *big, hairy, audacious goals*. Not just your regular, garden-variety goals. No, sir. They are goals with gumption, targets you can't wait to hit and will take your life to stratospheric levels. I can't wait to hit any of my goals, but BHAGs are truly life changing.

For example, a goal I tend to see is "Get in shape." It's okay, as goals go, but it's not particularly a SMART goal and not one that inspires me to get moving now (which is what a "get in shape" kinda goal is supposed to do, right?). A SMART and super-inspiring BHAG would be more like this, "I am in the best shape of my life: I weigh 180 pounds and have 13 percent body fat." When spiffed up, the goal of "I want to increase my billable hours" becomes: "I double my billing. I bill in excess of $20,000 per month in fees, for a total of $65,000 in 100 days."

Your Goal Setting Exercise

Now is the time for the rubber to meet the road. Pull out your vision, purpose, and plan, and review them thoroughly. Then set some BHAGs you can't wait to start achieving by using these steps:

1. Pretend today is your day one. For at least 20 minutes, brainstorm a list of everything you want to achieve over the next 100 days.

2. Review your list and circle your top three to five items (three if you're using my 100-day plan).

3. Write down the kind of person it will take to achieve all that you want. Describe character traits, values, beliefs, virtues, and so forth that this person (you!) would embody. List these characteristics under your Empowering Descriptors.

Committed or Just Excited?

Goals don't exist just for the sake of achieving something. Goals help us to become all we're meant to be. They help us find out what we're made of and discover our true capabilities. The fastest path to an achieved goal is the path you're committed to taking.

Goals are especially important as you navigate the unchartered territory after your divorce. Any residual anger, sadness, or low self-esteem can keep you stuck, whereas some cleverly set goals can catapult you in a more positive direction.

Let's complete the circle of goal setting. I want you to do one more exercise.

•   Write a paragraph about why you're committed to achieving each goal you have set.

Not just why you want to achieve it, but why you're *committed* to achieving it. Life in general can be hard, even harsh at times. After a divorce, well, forget about it! Life can be downright awful. When you feel like you're doing everything within your power and making no progress whatsoever, refer to these paragraphs about your commitment. They will stand as mile markers on your goal highway, enabling you to overcome any resistance you have to continuing forward and see again and again *why* you want your *what*.

Remember this: In a dish of ham and eggs, the chicken is interested, but the pig is committed. In this scenario, you are the pig. The pig sacrifices everything to become your dinner; the chicken provides a little something on the side. If you genuinely must achieve your goals, then you must be absolutely 100 percent committed. You are unquestionably committed to making your goals come true, right? I know you are!

You've done a lot of work—congratulations! You've set some goals that will inspire you to do the necessary work to achieve them. The person you're becoming as a newly-single person is quite remarkable—in fact, don't be surprised if you get some positive remarks about your transformation starting anytime now.

Now you have some BHAGs! I'm excited for you! If you haven't already, head on over to HonoreeCorder.com/Resources (use the password *success*) and download the free 100-day plan. Using the goals you've set, you'll create your initial 100-day plan by employing almost exactly the same process you used to create your longer-term plan, only of course your timeline is now much tighter.

You should be able to easily create a solid, inspiring plan that will get and keep you moving forward! Which means it's time to ...

Moving On:
Your Action Steps for Moving Forward

✓ Set some goals!

✓ Make sure they are BHAGs (at least some of them).

✓ Commit 100%.

Chapter Seven:
Dating after Divorce
for Fun and for Love

All of the good ones are taken. Not true.

No one wants to be with a single dad of three. Not true.

All men want are 25-year-olds with perfect bodies and lots of free time. Also not true.

There is nothing like a divorce to cause one to take stock of what they *really* want in a relationship. From *I don't ever want to be with someone who doesn't make their own money* to *I'd love someone who could pick up after themselves at least once!* The list of must haves and must not haves can range from the general and broad to the intensely specific.

The exercises in this chapter will help you to get as much clarity about who you want to spend all (or some) of the rest of your life with as you've gotten from doing your visions and plans. But before we go too far down that road, let's start in a happy place: your happy future.

I remember one of my girlfriends saying to me, "Friends are great and all, Honorée, but I want love! How do I find someone new to share my life with?"

You, too, might be wondering if it is possible for you to find a new and wonderful love. I have just one word for you: *yes!*

Remember the life lesson from the last chapter about being authentically yourself? Well, the lesson was one of the first gifts my husband gave me. Not only is it great for friendships, it will work wonders for your love life, too.

After we had been dating awhile, he asked why I barely kissed him on our first date. I told him that I had done that (and, ahem, more) on first dates before, and clearly I was still single. I wanted to do things differently, especially because I'd had time to think, reflect, and get a clear picture about what I truly wanted. I wanted a different result from dating, and by golly, I was going to do something different to get that result.

My husband is truly a man's man. He's confident, secure, and smart. He was raised by a single mom, a confident, secure, and smart career woman. Because he was raised so well, his opinion is solid, and I really admire him and trust what he has to say. He was *the first man* I had known to say what he meant, mean what he said, and do what he said he was going to do. His consistent, and congruent behavior really got my attention.

Now back to our discussion. Once I shared my reluctance on that first date, he said, "Honey, you can't do the wrong thing with the right man. He went on to explain: A real man can tell who you are, knows you're a good person, and won't judge you for what you do or don't do."

Wow. How refreshing! Where had this man been all of my life?

He continued. "So, whatever you really wanted to do on our first date, I would've been game." (*Smile.*) Did I mention he's funny, too?

Since that conversation, I've asked lots of men whose opinions I trusted if what my husband said is true, and all of them concurred 100 percent. For you male readers, I'd love for you to weigh in.

The general consensus is that men want to be with, and are really attracted to, women who are confident and happy. The opposite is also true:

There is nothing more attractive than a confident, kind man.

New Love Starts Here

What better memory to look back upon than the time you met your new love? Your last first date, the one where you realized you'd been through the fire, healed the wounds and scars, and knew it was all worth it because the person by your side is the person you'd waited all your life to find?

What if I told you everything you've been through in your life is leading you directly to *that person*, the one who will love you in a way you've never been loved, supports you in a way you've never experienced (but totally deserve), and will put a lot of your recent experiences into perspective? I just did, and I believe it's true with all of my heart.

Let me tell you why: My life today, my career, where I live, my family and friends, even this book you're holding, is a result not only of my divorce, but also the person I became after my divorce ... All of which allowed me to meet and attract the wonderful man I am married to today. If it sounds like I'm still basking in the glow of new love, I promise you I am not. As I write this, my husband and I just celebrated the eighth anniversary of the night we met. Far better, I think, than the euphoric rush of a new relationship, is the deep and rich love of a mature and happy one.

How did I get from there (divorced, single mom) to here (happy, remarried mom)? Instead of telling you more of my story, I'm going to guide you through exercises to get you started on creating yours.

Do a Relationship Review

I hope by now you've fallen truly, madly and deeply in love with you ... That would be truly fantastic! You're either ready to fall in love again, could entertain the idea, or are at least open to dating. Well, dating is where it all starts, so no matter what, you're at least *ready enough*.

Before I help you find love after divorce, I want you to keep in mind if you keep doing what you've always done, you're going to keep getting what you've always gotten.

That's great if you what you've been getting has been fantastic and you want more of it. But if you're reading this book, then you have at least one undesirable relationship in your past, you're single, and you want something better for yourself.

Fair enough.

The first step toward finding love is to look into your past and do a review of your marriage. Moving forward happens much more easily when you have obtained the clarity that can come only from looking in to the past. While the past does not equal the future— thank goodness! —what you learn about yourself by taking the time to do a relationship review can be a determining factor in the decisions you make in the future.

Being cautious and insightful works both ways. If your past has been particularly hurtful and painful, you can be, will be, and should be more cautious in your future actions. On the contrary, sometimes what has happened in the past can inspire you to be bolder or more carefree in your decisions. Truly, each of the characters of your life, male or female, has influenced how you respond or react to future situations.

Remember my Lessons Learned List? This list might reveal things about your relationship (positive and not so positive) that might not otherwise occur to you.

It is a good idea to see if you can identify the lessons from your prior marriage. If nothing else, it can help you to put some of the relationship into perspective, arm you with knowledge about yourself, and perhaps help you heal on an entirely new level. When you identify these takeaways, you're more likely to get them, which in turn will allow you to get something better and different in your new relationship(s).

Here is an example of a Lessons Learned List from a participant in the *Single Mom Transformation Program*:

- It's important not to force anything—ever.

- My relationships should (must! will!) be mutually beneficial, loving, etc.—give and expect to receive, too.

- I will follow my intuition; it always serves me.

- I will notice the signs—not ignore them because I don't want to see them.

- I will keep my son out of the equation until I'm sure the person I'm dating going to be around for the long haul.

- Take it s-l-o-w.

- A mutually-beneficial relationship requires me to be a whole person with another whole person, and ...

- ... it should be fun and fabulous with lots of giggling, laughing, and fantastic sex.

Through the process of creating this list, she learned some interesting things about herself and what she tended to do and what she allowed to happen in her relationships. Once she saw her patterns in black and white, the aha! moments were quick and gave almost instant clarity. She could not deny that she needed to raise her standards and give herself some new guidelines for future relationships and her behavior in connection with them.

There is no right or wrong way to write your list. If you haven't already done this exercise, set aside at least twenty minutes to identify and connect with the lessons you were meant to learn and the blessings that will result in your life because you have taken them to heart.

Based on your lessons learned, you can now identify on a deeper level how you would like to behave in the future, how you would like your partner to behave, and what you simply won't allow to happen again. This is also known as loving yourself, which in turn sets a fantastic example for your kids or anyone else who happens to watch your every move.

In order to cleanly move forward, your Lessons Learned List can, and most definitely should, include what you've learned about you, the choices you've made, and the reactions you've had. From those insights, you can choose what you want to be different about you and your life in the future.

I don't believe either party is 100 percent responsible for the beginning, middle, or end of a relationship. What I do believe is that if I take 100 percent of the responsibility, I leave no opportunity to place blame. Then, and only then, there can be no victim. I could say only that I chose him, I chose the relationship, or I made the decision to stay. Then I can also say, "I can choose something better, and I'm going to choose something better in the future."

But before we can choose to have something new, there's a very important step to complete. If you try to skip this step, you will likely end with your heart broken or, at the very least, hurt again. Therefore, with an open mind and heart, read on!

Here's your new dating process:

1. Identify the type of person you'd like to date and why you're dating.

2. State your purpose for dating all the time (tell everyone!).

3. Have fun and enjoy the process.
4. Have no expectations.
5. Don't be attached to the outcome.

Let me break these down and explain them further.

Decide What You Want: What's Your Purpose for Dating?

My philosophy on the art of dating is quite simple:

Dating is an opportunity to ask for what you want, say what you're looking for (your purpose for dating), date lots of people (as many as you'd like), have fun and enjoy the process, have almost no expectations, and remain unattached to the outcome.

When you follow my philosophy, you actually stand a better chance of ending up with the person who is the best fit for you, sooner. Much sooner.

The process for dating is relatively simple, and it starts with you deciding, before you go on your next date, why you're dating.

Do you want to have fun? Companionship? Find someone to marry?

If the perfect person to date were to walk into your life, what would they be like, and *why would they be there?* Take some time to list what you want from dating and what the person or people would be like that you'd be dating. Let me share an example.

"I want a mutually-beneficial, monogamous relationship with my best friend. He needs to be up to big things because I'm up to big things, and we will cheer each other on, share victories, challenges, and love. We can get married, or not, have children, or not. He must be a great "bonus dad" to my daughter, and I will be an amazing wife or partner for him."

You guessed it. That was my purpose for dating. And that is exactly who I married.

Ask for What You Want

There is someone out there who wants to receive what you want to give and who will give you what want you to receive.

Your role in this process is to identify what you want and speak your truth (state your dating purpose), to sort through the people you meet, and to continue sorting until you've found the person you're going to date, live with, marry, have children with, all of the above, or none of the above.

Oh yes, and you probably will want to enjoy the process. Therefore, decide right now that you're going to begin this process when, and only when, you can commit to yourself to enjoying the process and not before.

I make it sound so easy, right? Actually it's simple, but I recognize it's not necessarily easy because of the way we are wired and because of the way we're used to doing things.

State Your Purpose for Dating All the Time

I advise you state your purpose for dating all the time. Tell everyone within the sound of your voice what and who exactly you're looking to find. Anyone you tell may have a relative, co-worker, or neighbor who sounds like a good fit. You just never know where your next Ms. or Mr. Wonderful is going to come from. My husband and I met through a mutual friend. His former attorney is married to my one of my girlfriends. She and I met at a party and became fast friends. Once she realized I was single and asked what I was looking for, I told her. I told lots of other people, too, but she was the one who made the mental connection and the introduction.

If you're so inclined, add yourself to dating sites. These services automatically put you in front of people who are actually looking too, and they put right on their profile what they are looking to find. You can state exactly what you're looking for, and the right person will think that's really great and want to connect with you.

Remember this: you must **a-s-k** to **g-e-t.** All of the wishing and hoping from the comfort of your own home simply won't get you the love you want. Watching *Grey's Anatomy* will keep you current on the show, but it doesn't put you in front of potential love interests. You've got to meet new people to get love.

Have Fun and Enjoy the Process

What's the point if you don't have fun and enjoy the process? When all of your energy is wrapped up in finding, you won't be enjoying.

I have found that, in the process of dating, and even now (still) in the process of building my businesses, that staying in a state of curiosity is your best bet for enjoying the process. When I meet new folks, I'm curious about what makes them tick, what they're passionate and excited about, and why they think they're on this planet. Not everyone is a good fit as a friend or client, but everyone has a story, and I want to know it. Make discovering the stories of the people you're dating part of your dating process. Even if the two of you are not a good romantic fit, you could find some really cool, interesting people who might turn out to be great friends.

Inject fun into your dating life. Go to new restaurants, indulge in new foods, try miniature golfing, go hiking, learn how to stand-up paddle, learn a new language, train for a triathlon, etc. All of these activities put you in front of people, many of them new-to-you people.

My suggestion is to make a list of restaurants where you want to eat, activities you want to try, and places you want to visit. Then, start doing. Check out your list of thing you want to be, do, and have and incorporate them into this list as well. Work your way down your list, all the while adding new activities. You will even have an alternate use for this list in the dating process (stay tuned).

I had a blast joining new groups, making new friends, and learning about new things during my single years. An added bonus is that you can make friends with as many people of both sexes as you want. I have many male friends, all of whom I made when I was single. Relationships with the opposite-sex are generally not encouraged when you're in a relationship, but if you make them now, the added bonus is not just those relationships, but also the fact that those relationships become part of the package that is you.

Have No Expectations

"Is he the one?!" "Is HE the one?!" "IS HE THE ONE?!?!" Lather. Rinse. Repeat.

I have heard a lot of people (mostly women, to be fair) asking themselves this question very early, even before the first date, when they've connected with a "live one."

When you have high expectations that are placed on one potential mate, the chances of those expectations being met are indeed slim. He (or she) could be "the one" (one of many), but chances are, they will be another opportunity to refine your desires, get better at dating, have a great time, and meet a cool, new person.

Or, they could be your Ms. or Mr. Wonderful, and if they could be and you're in a state of "IS-S/HE-THE-ONE" panic mode, you'll most likely scare them off. I had more than one guy talk about marriage or the benefits of his job on our first date. Seriously? Too soon everyone!

Can you imagine going on a date with the only expectation being that you're going to have a conversation (maybe even a good one) and a nice meal? Wouldn't that take the frenetic energy out of the date? The energy that holds *expectation and hope* and even a little bit of crazy? Wouldn't that be nice? Yes, yes it would. Nod and smile, so I know you're with me, okay?

Dating is supposed to be fun. Repeat after me: **Dating is fun.**

Meeting someone new is going to be *fun*. Stating your purpose for dating is going to be *fun*. Eating out is going to be *fun*. Having some grown-up, non-children time is going to be *fun*. An evening out is a blast if, at the end of it, you actually want to go on another date!

Do yourself and your sanity a favor and detach yourself from expectations. Before you go on each date, remind yourself that in order to have fun, the best expectation is no expectation. That way, you will be pleasantly surprised when, eventually, something great does happen, and you meet your Mr. or Ms. Wonderful.

Don't Be Attached to the Outcome

My friend, Beth, who introduced me to my husband, had tried to get us together for months. I was very happily single, working on my businesses, and raising my daughter. I was so unattached to the outcome, that I (incorrectly) predicted the outcome of our first date. I told her to have no expectations because when I "didn't fall in love with him and marry him" I didn't want her to be upset or disappointed.

I was so not into finding someone that I went on a date almost against my will. I was completely uninterested. I'm sure you've heard the saying, "When you least expect it, expect it." That was me. I didn't expect it, even though I was clear on my purpose for dating; therefore, in a way, I was asking for it, and that's when it happened.

It's up to you to speak your purpose for dating, go on dates, have a great time (even if the person you're with is not having a great time with you), and go on your merry way. If they call again, great. If you end up together *forever*, terrific! If you don't, just keep on keepin' on.

Your outcome is your purpose for dating: That's the Big Outcome you want to have happen at the right time in the future. In the meantime, you're working, caring for your kids if you have them, making new friends, and creating an incredible future. Right? Right!

The Dating Challenge

Following all five steps in the dating process will require courage, for it takes courage to do something new and different to get new and different results.

I'm going to challenge you to do just that: something different. Maybe many things different. If you usually go on a date and get into a relationship, try going on a half-dozen dates with the same person before you commit and take yourself off the market.

If you've had three first dates and three relationships, take the plunge into the deep end of the pool and go on ten first dates. If you think you have to dress a certain way, and that way isn't you in your fullest sense, wear what makes you the most comfortable and attractive *to yourself*. Remember, you're most attractive to others when you're authentically yourself and most attractive to yourself.

Do the thing that scares you the most when it comes to dating. Shake things up. Shake yourself up! You deserve to try something new and get a new, great result.

Sort!

Going on lots of dates is simply sorting. You're sorting through the possibilities to find someone who is a perfect fit for you. There are so many people, you couldn't possibly date them all before finding a companion who makes you feel amazing. There are *billions* of people on this planet, so that means there are literally hundreds of people, if not thousands, who would be a great fit for you. If you haven't identified some new prospects, you don't have a finding problem, you have a sorting problem.

Perhaps it's a good idea to decide, right now, to date one hundred people in the next year. Too many? Okay, then what's your number? When you have a big enough number and you keep it in mind, you'll be more apt to remember you're *sorting* and be open to trying out lots of potential mates before settling on one.

Speak Your Truth

When you are dating, you have the perfect opportunities to speak your truth, whatever that is. You're a single mom or dad, a two-time divorcée, excited about your career or the new business you want to start, or going back to school, and you're dating because [insert your purpose for dating here].

Remember the part about becoming attractive to others by first becoming attractive to yourself? Part of that attractiveness is speaking your truth. Sharing is how people connect, and it's no different during the dating process.

Save Yourself for the Best Fit (aka You Deserve the Best!)

This part is where I insist that you not settle. Good enough is just not good enough.

This process isn't about finding Ms. or Mr. Perfect. They simply do not exist. This process is about finding Ms. or Mr. Perfect-For-You. My husband isn't perfect (pretty darn close), but he is perfect for me. We complement each other so well, and that makes our relationship harmonious (most days, anyway). I'm so clear about the fact that I'm not perfect, but he swears I'm perfect for him. That's a pretty great feeling, a feeling you, too, deserve to have.

I always say it's better to be single and happy than to be in a relationship and miserable. Because you're divorced, I'm sure that right about now you're nodding your head. Don't settle, and you won't end up divorced or on the other side of a broken relationship again wishing you hadn't.

Dating is pressure and tension. What is a date, really, but a job interview that lasts all night? —Jerry Seinfeld

Have you ever seen two people who desperately wanted to make each other happy, and each of them got it almost right? You could see where they were just missing the mark in making the right connection, so it didn't work out, and neither of them knew exactly why?

Well, that's what happens between men and women when they're dating and in relationship all the time.

He Wants to Make You Happy. You Want to Make Him Happy. So, What's the Problem?

The best way for him to make you happy is for him to give you exactly what you want, take you exactly where you want to go, and share the exact experiences you want.

The best way for you to make him happy is for you to tell him what you want, where you want to go, and what you want to experience. But how many times have the wires been crossed and that's not what happened? Let me show you how this works.

When my husband and I went on a lunch date to celebrate our fourth anniversary, we were the perfect example of this typical "we want to please each other challenge," even though we know each other very well.

We got in the car, and he said, "Where would you like to go?"

Well, I like Austin-centric places that serve brown rice and tofu, but I knew he wouldn't like that, so I said, "Doesn't matter. Where would you like to go?"

He replied, "You're driving, so I want to go anywhere you want to go."

Then, I said, "You don't want to go anywhere I'd like to go because I know you wouldn't want to go to Which Wich."

He agreed. We went back and forth for five minutes while I was driving to "wherever," and I finally said, "Let's go to The Domain to The Steeping Room. If you don't like the menu, which he didn't, we'll find another place to go." We ended up somewhere, but it took a whole lot of energy and time, even though we know each other really well!

Here's why we struggle:

Note: What I'm talking about in this section are masculine and feminine energies. Typically a relationship has one person embodying either masculine or feminine energy. I'm using the terms "men" and "women" to indicate these energies, regardless of which gender plays that role. If you want more detailed information, check out David Deida's *Intimate Communion* or Alison Armstrong's *In Sync with the Opposite Sex*.

Men are providers.

Men want to provide the experience that makes you happy. A man's instinct is to be a provider and protector, and he is seeking to provide for his woman.

Men are hunters.

This same man has one, single focus at a time, and he must focus to get things done in order to produce a result. Note: he always has a result to produce.

Men disconnect in order to stay focused.

Men disconnect from women and from everything except their singular focus, not because they don't like the person they are with, but because, yes, you guessed it, he's producing a result.

Men like to be in control.

Men do not like to be out of control. They want to be in control so they can provide the experience that makes the person he's with happy. (Sound familiar?)

On the other hand ...

Women are pleasers.

Women don't want to appear too demanding, so we pretend that we are easy-peasy, go-with-the-flow, and low-maintenance. We want those around us to be happy, and we think we are accomplishing that by deferring our own desires.

Women are gatherers and connectors.

Women have diffuse awareness, which means we can multitask, find what's right, and find what we're looking for. We use our innate "scan-vision," which allows us to maintain connections to others and what we're mainly focusing on while doing other things. We can and do stay connected to those around us even while we're doing a multitude of other tasks.

Women are nurturers.

Women nurture people. We are natural cultivators, developers, and supporters. We cherish our loved ones and do everything in our power to make them happy, as soon as possible and as often as possible.

What Does This Mean?

Because men are inherently physically stronger and women are inherently physically weaker, we are each wired and have roles that were biologically predetermined for us. Men are the providers and protectors. They are wired to provide for us and to protect us. Women are pleasers because of the biological dependency we are wired to have on men; therefore, women seek to please men, and the truth is we are obsessed with pleasing men. All of our instincts tell us that we are to please a man, and in return, he will provide and protect us.

I'm not saying men and women are this way in today's society, I'm saying this is how we are biologically wired. In today's world, there are many women who out-earn men and actually provide for them. I'm just conveying what the research says about how we're biologically built. When we know more information, we can use that information to make our lives better.

Here's why this is a problem when we're dating:

For example, when a man asks us what we want to eat, what we want to do for fun, where we want to go, we want to please him, so we say, "Anything is fine." Just like for my anniversary date. I knew we were not communicating well while it was happening, and I still couldn't quite figure out how to navigate the situation perfectly.

Ladies, your date wants to provide for you what will make you happy, so when you say, *Anything is fine*, he's actually frustrated because he doesn't know what to do to make you happy. So he takes you to the last place where someone looked happy. Of course going where he's been with someone else would be upsetting to us because we don't want to go where "she" (whoever she was) has been. He doesn't know what you like because you said, "Anything is fine," so he is actually hoping you'll like what someone else seemed to like. Make sense? You would be far better off to decide in advance a whole bunch of different things you'd like to do, so when he asks, you're ready!

If you think about it for a minute, you do have an opinion about what you like and don't like, right, ladies? Didn't we discuss this topic in an earlier chapter when you were getting busy falling in love with you? You did make that list of things you wanted to do, to learn, places you wanted to eat, to go and see? That list is going to come in handy while you're dating, too, because you can go to it when the man-of-the-moment says, *What would you like to have when we go to dinner?* Now is your chance to use this previously discovered information to help your date make you happy!

Gentlemen, your antidote to, "Anything is fine," is to make a plan based on what you know about her (she's vegan, don't go to Ruth's Chris) or ask. *Is there any particular restaurant you've been meaning to try out?* If you get, "Anything is fine!" then say, "I was thinking of taking us to this really cool Cuban-Chinese restaurant on the Upper West Side. Have you heard of it? How does that sound?" Women love a decisive man, especially a courteous one.

There is so much great information about love, dating, and relationships. I've shared only the tip of the iceberg. Check out anything by Alison Armstrong, particularly her audio program *In Sync with the Opposite Sex*. She is full of enlightening information.

Enjoy!

If you follow my suggestion of disconnecting from expectations and have fun and enjoy the process, your dating life could (and dare I say should) be much more enjoyable than the last time you found yourself in the dating world.

> *Life is either a daring adventure or nothing.*
> —Helen Keller

Moving On:
Your Action Steps for Moving Forward

✓ Do your Relationship Review and create a new or add to your Lessons Learned List.

✓ Define your Purpose for Dating and start telling *everyone*.

✓ Enjoy the process!

The Divorced Phoenix

Chapter Eight:
Wanderlust and Wonderment

We travel, some of us forever, to seek other states, other lives, other souls.
—Anaïs Nin

It doesn't matter where you are in your transformation, at some point, you will most likely be overcome with a strong desire to see what you haven't seen, meet who you haven't met, and go where you haven't gone before, only to discover, uncover, and live in a perpetual state of surprise. I believe these urges are aptly named *wanderlust* and *wonderment*.

And they are defined as ...

Wanderlust is a strong desire for or impulse to wander or travel and explore the world.

Wonderment is a state of awed admiration or respect.

It is my deepest hope that my words have provided you with the hope that your best days are yet to come, the knowledge and insight for how to navigate your new life, and the inspiration to fully embrace your transformation. In case you still need a little something, a nudge, a hug, a push, allow me to provide all of the above in the form of stories of those who have engaged in their own transformations—and won!

I asked three questions of people I knew who had not only survived their divorce, but were living happy, fulfilling lives in which they were thriving.

Question 1: Do you think your life is better or worse since your divorce? Explain.

Absolutely better! I no longer live in fear. I have blossomed! I am more outgoing and happier. I am a better parent and a more loving person. I am not afraid of taking chances. I know that even the most awful things will pass if you just keep moving forward. —Francine Roling

My life is WAY better! I don't have to clean up after anyone. I don't have to answer to anyone, cover, or make excuses as to why I can't be somewhere—because the tension was so high between us all the time. I am now in control of my finances, which have fluctuated over the years, but I've always had more than enough, and I don't have any credit card debt. I'm free to be me! —Janet Eddy

Far better. I have an excellent career, I remarried and have a great family, and my relationship with my son is exceptionally strong because I have always supported his relationship with his mother. —Martin Smith

WAY better. From the day we agreed to divorce, I could breathe again, and my life was instantly better. No regrets whatsoever. —Wendy Williams

It's definitely better. I am much more empowered and have been promoted in my career. My salary has grown, and I own another business. I have a hobby I enjoy, along with friends that I don't have to hide from since my ex hated my friends. One of those friends whom my ex didn't allow me to talk to—we are still friends to this day. —Heather Buen

My life has changed dramatically for the better. I'm living in a place I love, married to a man I love, doing work I love. I have the children I always wanted. I am a better version of me. —Sarah Atlas

My life is much better now than before I was divorced. Though it was painful and scary to take that big leap, it has allowed me to move from a bleak existence where I wasn't excited about anything in my life to a plain full of possibilities. When I reached my 30th birthday and asked, *Is this all there is?* I needed to make big changes. I'm so happy and grateful that I did.—C. Penwell

Question 2: What does your life look like now, and would any of these things have occurred if you had stayed married?

I am stable financially. My ex-husband spent money foolishly and even forged my name before to buy things on credit, like some type of gun he had to have. I know how to budget my money, and I've been able to provide for my daughters. Even on a smaller increase, we've been able to travel and do fun things! There's also been a huge shift in my thinking. I attract good stuff now! I've had a Shaklee business, and when I was married, it went nowhere. Since divorcing and finding who I was meant to be, I have a successful business and lead a team of builders! I have found an amazing man who loves me for who I am. We married in June 2015, and it is so different to be married this time. My daughters were always my first priority during my divorce. They are the reason I decided to divorce. I didn't want them to think this is what marriage and love is supposed to look like. The divorce hurt them, but it also brought us closer and has helped them to become strong women in their own right. They are effective communicators, and kind-hearted women who are capable of accomplishing anything they set their minds too. —Francine Roling

I developed a thirst for knowledge after my divorce. I have now gotten my business management associate degree, human relations bachelor's degree, and my master's in counseling. Learning empowered me, and I loved gaining knowledge! Challenges now energize me—both personally and professionally. I finally learned what my purpose in life is, which is counseling others. Helping people through tough times and empowering them to be the best version of themselves is now what I do everyday. I am now extremely blessed by my relationship with my daughter. I know we would not be as close had I stayed married. Our relationship morphed from a mother-daughter relationship to a mother-daughter-best friend relationship. Each and every job that I've had has led me to where I am now, and I am excited for the future! I finally realized that I can do anything I put my mind to! —Janet Eddy

I am remarried to a woman who is strong, intelligent, and supportive. Her children became the strong siblings for my son, and she an incredible stepmother. I have worked for 20 years at the same company and have an excellent career at a place that is very family oriented. Naturally there have been ups and downs like with everyone else in the world, but with this family has always persevered. This couldn't have happened without being with someone who is such an excellent individual as well as partner. It also wouldn't have happened without the divorce. It's unfortunate, but we were young and idealistic which means we were also completely UNrealistic about who we were. —Martin Smith

As soon as we agreed to divorce, he said he would move out. So I packed my bag and stayed with a friend for the weekend so that my husband could take whatever belongings he wanted. I didn't care about "stuff." When I returned, hardly anything was gone, but I immediately made plans to live life, meet people, go line dancing, become a nude model for extra money, take on a new career as a real estate agent (at that time), and really enjoy sex. I did all of those things and was so happy! Since then, I became an executive assistant in the wine industry, but am now self-employed as The Cleanup Queen (I own my own residential/commercial cleaning business), which I love, have married a man whom I've been friends with since 1983, recently wrote a book on Amazon ... Hmmm, I'm just generally a positive, happy person and love my life even more. We moved to Southern California a year ago and moved into our dream house in our dream town, and I probably wouldn't be here if I had remained married. I must say, my ex remarried a lovely woman who was a wonderful and loving stepmother to my daughter, and my ex and I (through his wife) remained on friendly terms and continued to get together at special events for the sake of our daughter. I wouldn't have changed a thing! I really learned that sometimes two people just aren't meant to be together long-term—it wasn't one person's fault. That's when I knew I had to get divorced. —Wendy Williams

My life today has its own ups and downs, but I truly believe that I would have never started my own business or tried freelance writing while being married to my ex. I would have never taken a risk in my career by which I have gained so much: knowledge, insight, mentors, and friendship. Since my marriage I have paid off my debts and cleaned up my credit. Personally I feel a lot more confident about myself and definitely a lot more sexy. Today I am a blogger and freelance writer. I also work at UT Arlington as an adjunct professor teaching web marketing and Google Analytics. I write for CBS, Examiner.com, and ACX.com among other publications. I am truly grateful for the experiences I have had being my own boss. —Heather Buen

I am in a stable and loving relationship that is a true partnership. I have left a job that made me feel miserable and traded it for really cup-filling work that I love doing and am good at. I have beautiful children. I am grateful every day for the changes that came about as a result of my divorce. I no longer hide myself from the world; I'm not afraid to be the most me version of me. That's a gift. – Sarah Atlas

Before I was divorced, I had no friends outside of work. I didn't go places other than to run errands, and I didn't do anything for fun other than read escapist romance novels. I never traveled except to see family. Today, I have a loving husband, rambunctious children, and a bunch of dear friends. I do work that makes me excited to get out of bed in the morning with people who challenge and enrich my life. I travel to see family, but also take trips just for the adventure. —C. Penwell

Question 3: I asked what advice they would give themselves "if they knew then what they know now," and, as luck would have it, their answers are nothing short of transformational!

Everyone is not your friend! People like to gossip, and they don't understand divorce. Most are afraid of divorce, and so they make assumptions. They want to think this can't happen to them. This is your journey, and only you need to understand it. There's no right or wrong way to do it. It's individual. Spend quiet time each day so you can hear your heart. All tough times do pass. As long as you do something, you won't feel stuck. Keep a journal so you can see how far you've come. Surround yourself with people you love and trust, those who don't judge. This doesn't have to be a large number but you do need a posse. You need adults in your life whom you can vent to so you don't slip and say anything to your kids. Lastly, as painful as it may be, embrace this metamorphosis. Find the positive so you don't become negative and bitter. —Francine Roling

That everything was going to be okay. I would tell myself, "You're not a failure. Always,

always, always listen to your heart, your mind, and your gut. You know what is best deep down." I would tell myself, "You did the best you could at the time with your daughter. You'll make some incredibly good choices, and some mistakes, but every parent makes mistakes. Your daughter will grow up to be an amazing woman, and you will be just fine. And someday there will come a time that you will need your daughter, and she will be there for you." Most importantly, "Stay positive. At all times, stay positive because negativity begets negativity."
—Janet Eddy

Sometimes life is a giant ball of shit, and you just have to keep at it until it is better. Be vigilant that your child never hears you speak poorly of the other parent ... But do not be a doormat, either. Your main job is to make that child feel loved by you, AND by the other parent, even when it makes you want to vomit in your mouth a little. (Which I generally did quite successfully ... thanks to my current wife).
—Martin Smith

To be flexible and not let pride get in the way. Especially when children are involved, it's best to LISTEN to the other person, acknowledge, and then "bend" here and there. Both my ex and I learned this. Everything was "as the divorce decree says ..." until we both realized that life isn't always black and white and that in order for everyone to be happy, we need to be flexible, to give and take. I wish I could have learned this earlier on in the process so that the divorce would have taken six months instead of two years. Ultimately, everything turned out very well. —Wendy Williams

I would tell myself to not be afraid of things that are unknown. I used to be afraid of things that were nothing to be afraid of. During the divorce and in the aftermath my ex has done everything to keep me down, including disappearing, not paying child support, sending disparaging emails about me to potential partners and sponsors, and I have come through all of that via my own personality and actions. I may not have been perfect, but I believed in myself and many great things happened in spite of his jealousy and anger. Always keep your head high and keep your goals clear. Nothing can stand in the way of your goals except yourself. —Heather Buen

I'd give myself permission to put myself first earlier in my life. I'd be better at going for what *I* wanted. –Sarah Atlas

I'd tell myself to be brave and willing to take the next step for yourself. Don't wait for someone or something to come along and save you. —C. Penwell

As you can see, your new life after divorce can eclipse your previous married life in just about every way. The sky is your limit, and all you have to do from this point forward is put one foot in front of the other.

You've got this! Cheers to your amazing new life!

Get Even More

AS A THANK YOU FOR reading this book, I want to give you a ***free* copy** of:

If Divorce is a Game, These are the Rules
8 Rules for Thriving Before, During and After Divorce

This book is packed with advice for anyone coping with a nasty divorce who wants to learn the secrets of a divorce where everyone wins. Go here and tell me where to send your free ebook:

http://honoreecorder.com/DivorceBook/

Gratitude

To Byron—I couldn't do any of this without your love and support. Thank you and I love you!

To Lexi—I'm blessed and grateful to be your mom every single day.

To my assistant Christina, whose brilliance sparkles every day! I am so grateful for you!

To the incredible individuals who made writing and publishing this book possible: the Divorced Phoenixes who allowed me to interview them for this project, my editing team Alyssa and Leslie, and Dino for designing this and all of my gorgeous book covers ... thank you, thank you!

Who Is Honorée

Honorée Corder is the best-selling author of more than a dozen books, including

If Divorce is a Game, These are the Rules;

Prosperity for Writers: A Writer's Guide to Creating Abundance;

Prosperity for Writers Productivity Journal: A Writer's Workbook for Creating Abundance;

Business Dating: Applying Relationship Rules in Business for Ultimate Success;

Vision to Reality: How Short Term Massive Action Equals Long Term Results;

The Successful Single Mom book series;

The Successful Single Dad;

Play2Pay;

Paying4College: How to Save 25-50% on Your Child's College Education;

Tall Order! Organize Your Life and Double Your Success in Half the Time.

She is also a serial entrepreneur, keynote speaker, and executive coach. She empowers others to dream big, clarify their vision, and turn that vision into reality.

Find out more at HonoreeCorder.com

Honorée Enterprises, LLC
Honoree@HonoreeCorder.com
http://www.HonoreeCorder.com
Twitter: @Honoree & @Singlemombooks
Facebook: http://www.facebook.com/Honoree
Instagram: @Honoree

Made in the USA
San Bernardino, CA
29 September 2016